FROM SERFDOM
TO SOCIALISM

FROM SERFDOM
TO SOCIALISM

J. KEIR HARDIE

Introduction by John Callow

London
Lawrence & Wishart 2015

Lawrence and Wishart Limited
99a Wallis Road
London
E9 5LN

This edition © GMB 2015

Published in association with the GMB

ISBN 978 1 910 448 472

Front Cover Top – Hardie photo: Wikimedia Commons;
red flag: Bigstock; collage: Lynette Williamson. Bottom: By
permission of East Ayrshire Leisure/East Ayrshire Council
Back Cover Top – courtesy ILP/WCML; Badge by permission of
East Ayrshire Leisure/East Ayrshire Council

British Library Cataloguing in Publication Data.
A catalogue record for this book is available from the British Library

FROM SERFDOM
TO SOCIALISM

J. KEIR HARDIE

Introduction by John Callow

London
Lawrence & Wishart 2015

Lawrence and Wishart Limited
99a Wallis Road
London
E9 5LN

ISBN 978 1 910 448 472

Front Cover Top – Hardie photo: Wikimedia Commons;
red flag: Bigstock; collage: Lynette Williamson. Bottom: By
permission of East Ayrshire Leisure/East Ayrshire Council
Back Cover Top – courtesy ILP/WCML; Badge by permission of
East Ayrshire Leisure/East Ayrshire Council

British Library Cataloguing in Publication Data.
A catalogue record for this book is available from the British Library

CONTENTS

... To fight,
Not in red coats against our brother man,
The pawns of Empire, or a despot's will,
But in grey lines of sober Brotherhood
Against the flaunting evils of the world,
The Cruelty that fastens on men's lives,
The dread brutality that hedges earth.
Come, ye that listen, rise and gird your swords,
Win back the fields of England for the poor,
Give roses to your children's fading cheeks,
And to the hearts of women hope again,
Bring back content unto the lives of men.

ABBREVIATIONS

GMB General, Municipal & Boilermakers Union
ILP Independent Labour Party
LRC Labour Representation Committee
PLP Parliamentary Labour Party
SDF Social Democratic Federation
TUC Trade Union Congress
WLL Women's Labour League
WSPU Women's Social and Political Union

ACKNOWLEDGEMENTS

The idea for this reprint originated with Richard Leonard, the GMB's Political Officer for Scotland and Chair of the Keir Hardie Society. Without his belief, enthusiasm and wide range of contacts, this book could never have existed in its current form. A similar debt of gratitude is owed to Cath Speight, GMB's National Political Officer, who understands the value of history – and of knowing precisely where you've come from – and the importance of projecting the essence of Keir Hardie's politics into the fight for radical change in the present day.

Lynette Cawthra and Jane Taylor at the Working Class Movement Library in Salford have been, as always, extremely helpful in providing access to images, books and journals. The WCML is a treasure trove for the British Labour Movement and it is good to know that the work of Eddie and Ruth Frow is being so ably, efficiently and faithfully carried on.

At the Baird Institute, Cumnock, which houses the largest and most important museum collection of Keir Hardie materials and memorabilia, John Stanley was able to make available a selection of artefacts and papers, under his curatorship, for use in the book. In London, Lord Tom Sawyer – a former General Secretary of the Labour Party – lent an image from an archive built up as part of a life's work; while, in the North East, Davy Hopper and the Durham Miners Association were similarly generous in putting some of the wonderful paintings in their collection at our disposal, reflecting the pride, the life and the labour of their communities.

David Connolly of the ILP could not have been more generous, or helpful, in granting copyright for many of the photographs used within this book, and for Keir Hardie's original work. The ILP can be contacted via their main website: www.independentlabour.org.uk; or via their email address: info@independentlabour.org.uk. In a similar fashion, the Keir Hardie Society, which was established in August 2010, and aims 'to keep alive the ideas and promote the life and work of Keir Hardie', is open to all and may be found, on the web, at: keirhardiesociety.co.uk. Their email address is: keirhardiesociety@gmail.com.

The editor's thanks are also due, last but by no means least, to Andrew Corbett, who worked on the design of this book; and to Sally Davison, Director of Lawrence & Wishart Publishing, who – along with the juggling of deadlines, production-runs and the business of editing copy – has added her own chapter to the story of independent, radical publishing in Britain and helped to promote a vibrant, creative and heterogeneous range of authors and journals that aim to claim the new century for open and progressive politics, of which Hardie would surely have been proud.

This is only the third edition of this book but, on the centenary of Keir Hardie's death, he is still to be found engaged in the battle of ideas. Once formed, those ideas cannot simply be forgotten, locked away, or dressed up as an empty and outmoded dogma. Rather, they take on a life of their own – independently of their creators – and, like those first pebbles thrown out into the stream, you never quite know how far they will fall and scatter, where their concentric rings might spread, or what further chains of thought and action they might, in their turn, create.

A DIVINE DISCONTENT:

KEIR HARDIE AND THE GENESIS
OF BRITISH SOCIALISM

R AIN LASHED AGAINST the boards of the empty
summer house at Lochnorris: books and papers
abandoned. The bereaved family, left suddenly
with neither breadwinner nor savings, debated whether or
not to sell the possessions of the departed. Deprived of
their quarry, the flag-wavers, distributers of white feathers
and jingoistic copy editors moved on to other targets. The
toll of casualties in Flanders was running at more than
2000 dead and wounded per day, victories were hard to
come by, and the chivalric notion of war, in defence of
'gallant little Belgium', had long been buried among the
mud and the wire. Yet 'the roar and song of a war-mad-
dened people' had – for the moment, at least – drowned
out the voice of the Socialist, the pacifist and the pioneer.[1]

James Keir Hardie, the self-conscious champion of so
many unpopular causes, who had never flinched from
the prospect of standing alone, had been felled by the
murderous reality of war and by the gulf that separated
the words from the deeds of so many of his comrades.
High-sounding resolutions passed by Europe's Socialists
on the eve of the conflict gave way – in some cases almost

overnight – to celebrations of nation and empire, and the rush to vote through the war credits that would set the munitions factories humming and propel the troop trains towards the frontiers.[2] Not for the first – or last – time, the European working classes had reacted in a wholly unexpected manner, in a way that defied the expectations of Socialist theory and polemic: they had replaced calls for solidarity and brotherhood, in many cases, with an extreme violence and hatred born out of competing nationalisms. Amid the ruins of an international Labour Movement that had appeared poised to carry all before it, Fenner Brockway thought – with good reason – that Hardie had been 'killed by the War equally with any soldier on the front'.[3]

In Glasgow crowds of working women and men still jostled against damp chapel doors, anxious to pay their respects to their fallen leader. An old workman doffed his cap, a khaki clad soldier stood to attention. But the funeral somehow disappointed. It seemed unable to capture the essence and the significance of the man it had sought to honour. None of his political colleagues had felt equal to the task, and by default the oration was therefore given by a sympathetic local clergyman, A.M. Forson – who chose to ignore Hardie as trade unionist organiser, Socialist politician and opponent of war. Instead, in death, he was defined by his youthful activities in the Evangelical Union, and as a colourful figure of local – as opposed to national, or international – importance, a man who was significant for the moral, as opposed to the practical political, force of his arguments. Hardie was cast as idealist rather than materialist; Old Testament prophet as opposed to tribune of the organised working class; homespun reformist rather than social revolutionary. Turning away in disgust, John Bruce Glasier thought that they might as well have been burying the village grocer.[4]

Unfortunately, it was this picturesque and overly senti-mentalised image of Hardie that came to dominate considerations of his political reputation and official representation in Labour Party circles over most of the next seventy years, reaching its apogee in the pages of John Cockburn's *The Hungry Heart. A Romantic Biography of James Keir Hardie*, which was published in 1956 and served as the leading popular biography of the man and politician for more than a generation.[5] Moreover, it was an image that was strengthened by the collapse of the rival personality cults of Ramsay MacDonald and Philip Snowden, after their betrayals of the party in 1931 had caused them to be effectively airbrushed out of the Parliamentary Labour Party's pantheon of heroes. Hardie was, therefore, a symbol of unity and consistency, about whom all shades of Labour opinion might agree and rally at times of crisis. However, his increasing status as undis-puted founder and figurehead of the party came at a price, inasmuch as he was effectively de-politicised by the successive theorists and leaders of the British Labour Movement. The 'Man in the Cloth Cap' was in danger of becoming the kind of mute totem, cited but seldom under-stood – and certainly never read – that was mercilessly caricatured in the 1980s comedy series *Brass*, in which 'Red Agnes' Fairchild would genuflect at mention of his name, and confer upon or suddenly withdraw possession of his tattered headdress to her sons, on the basis of their 'correct' political and class conduct.[6] The tendency to mythologise Hardie could lead to parody, but perhaps made others feel a necessity to qualify their praise. G.D.H. Cole, writing in the early 1940s, considered that Hardie 'had a mind which generated only on a basis of practical experience: he was never a theorist, and never burdened himself with more theories than he could put to practical use'; while H.N. Brailsford, composing a tribute for the ILP shortly after Hardie's death, in 1915, sought to praise his 'daring aggressive spirit' and 'sensitiveness and noble pride', but sniffed that, after all: 'It was not intellect that led him'.[7] More damning still, in regards to his political acumen, was the verdict of Viscount Samuel, the former leader of the Liberal Party, who had known Hardie at Westminster, and judged that 'perhaps at bottom he was not really a politician at all; he was a prophet rather, with the soul of a poet'.[8]

This emphasis on Hardie as, at heart, a social reformer driven by a religious mysticism and calling, as opposed to an essentially Socialist theoretical conviction, was certainly appealing – and politically useful – to the right wing of the Labour Party in the wake of the Second World War, in its battle with the Bevanites who sat to its left. Consequently, for Hugh Gaitskell, speaking in 1956 – the year that Soviet Communism appeared to have been revealed as being fatally flawed through its violent suppression of Imre Nagy's government in Hungary – Hardie's vision of Socialism 'was deeply rooted in his Christianity', rather than in any appeal to Marxist, or even Marxian, theory. Utopias could wait, and political ideas – as opposed to policies – were to be distrusted as dangerous and alien to the make-up of the British Labour Movement. As a reassuring consequence, Keir Hardie was now to be defined as 'a practical reformer as well as a great idealist'.[9] By the early 1980s, as the Cold War threatened once more to go hot, and Labour seemed to be upon the verge of becoming a radical, and avowedly Socialist, party, committed to abandoning nuclear weapons, Hardie was even appropriated by the Evangelical right wing of the movement for Moral Re-Armament: he became *The Man They Could Not Buy*, in a play which stripped him of his Socialism, and emphasised his Christianity and charitable impulses, at the expense of his opposition to imperialism and war.[10]

For a long time Hardie remained unchallenged as the inspiration and ultimate source of political legitimacy for the PLP. Writing in 1987, Neil Kinnock was able to emphasise Hardie as 'a man with deep and steadfast concern for individual self-expression and human freedom – the values of democratic Socialism', a characterisation that neatly combined Hardie's appeal for both the nascent reformist wing of his party, who were prepared to accept the basic tenets of neoliberalism and come to terms with the free market, and its core supporters, rooted in the collectivism of the trade unions, who were increasingly on the back foot.[11] Tony Blair, as leader of the Opposition, hung a portrait of Keir Hardie upon his office wall, and considered that his 'steadfast courage and political radicalism have provided a role model for generations of Labour people'.[12] Despite this glowing restatement of the moral and political inspiration from Hardie that lay behind the party's endeavours, it is worth noting that Blair had chosen to replace Hardie's avowed Socialism – taken as a given by both Kinnock and Gaitskell – with the more nebulous term 'radicalism'.

Furthermore, he had used the past tense when discussing Hardie's importance and enduring achievements: he *had* provided Labour's inspiration. But would he continue to do so, as the party sought to celebrate all that appeared 'new' and fresh?

The answer appeared within the covers of the party's official history, published shortly before the election victory of May 1997, wherein Hardie's contribution to the development of the Labour Movement was marginalised.[13] For an illustrated popular history this was scholarly and well-considered; but, significantly, it was also a conscious and cleverly calculated attempt to revise the party's self-conception. For the first time, Ramsay MacDonald was largely rehabilitated within the Labour canon, largely at Hardie's expense; and the common early debts of both men to Liberalism were emphasised, to the detriment of any sense of their later shared embrace of Socialism. Thus, the reader is informed that 'Keir Hardie's reputation ... [for] leading Labour to the promised land is probably exaggerated'; and his career – which was barely considered in the text – was judged to have ended in abject failure.[14] Hardie had at last been toppled from his pedestal in the eyes of the Labour Movement. He now appeared to be an uncomfortable and even discordant figure for 'New' Labour, as the party leadership became comfortable with big business, the privatisation of state assets and the energetic prosecution of a series of adventurous – if spectacularly unsuccessful – foreign wars. Suddenly the prophet was without honour, or at least recognition, within his own land.[15]

That Hardie could be so thoroughly excised from Labour's collective memory was partly due to the failure of the left wing to take proper ownership of his legacy; and it was also partly because of the readiness with which the left had accepted the critique of its foes that Hardie was – at best – an organiser and propagandist, not a man who dealt with Socialist ideas in his own right. The combination of his fusty tweeds and evangelical religion seemed decidedly off-putting to the New Left and the counter-culture of the late 1960s and early 1970s; in their celebration – and virtual fetishisation – of theory and abstraction, they tended to view Hardie as the product, and possible progenitor, of the brand of 'Labourism' and dull reformism that had effectively prevented the development of an 'authentic' revolutionary party in the British Isles.[16] As a consequence, Hardie's apparent unwillingness to engage with theoretical questions was used as a stick to beat him with. One of his leading biographers, writing in 1975, dismissed him as 'not a profound thinker', while the introductory essay for the 1974 re-issue of *From Serfdom to Socialism* showed little sympathy either for Hardie's personal abilities or for the aims and achievements of the Labour Party itself.[17] Indeed, both Hardie and his book are treated in the harshest of terms and subjected to the most withering of critiques. 'There is not', we are told, 'a scrap of evidence in this volume that the intellectual leaders of the Labour Party were provided with any sharp or incisive tool of analysis of the social and intellectual ferment which Britain underwent from about 1905'. Hardie is viewed as boastful and limited, while his understanding of the term 'Socialism' is judged as being simply confined to 'an approval word used by good men to commend some of the past and to yearn for a better future'.[18] As a result: 'intellectually the version of

socialism advanced in this volume is not especially impres-
sive, coherent or even convincing'; and it is responsible for
'the unstructured and incoherent ideology of Labourism',
since 'literally, Labourism excludes nothing'.[19]

Given such a damning verdict by the editor of its last
edition, it might reasonably be wondered why the Keir
Hardie Society and the GMB trade union would have
taken the time and the trouble to re-issue *From Serfdom
to Socialism* in order to commemorate the centenary of
Hardie's death. The first reason for this move lies in a
desire to make Hardie's work – long out-of-print – available again, at a reasonable price, for a new generation of
political activists, trade unionists and grassroots members
of the Labour Party. They can then read for themselves
what Hardie actually wrote, rather than simply being
forced to accept received wisdoms about the nature and
qualities of his work, mediated at third or even fourth
hand. Secondly, the book stands as both the founding
document of the Labour Party and as the fullest exposition of Keir Hardie's political thought: significant reasons
in their own right. Unlike the majority of his other works,
it deals with core ideas and fundamental principles, as
opposed to campaigns and issues that dominated in their
own day (such as Labour's tortuous process of separation
from the Liberals, Indian independence, Irish Home Rule,
opposition to the Boer War, Temperance, land and tariff
reforms), but which are of historical, as opposed to immediate, importance in ours.[20] A bestseller on its original
publication in 1907, *From Serfdom to Socialism* was a
seminal text for the first generation of ILP activists; and it
sought to draw together Hardie's often disparate ideas –
on history, religion, women's suffrage and rights, and

local and national government – into a coherent and explicitly Socialist whole. When the book was first published – in marked contrast to its later reception in the 1970s – it was lauded by Hardie's friends and supporters for its 'charm' and 'lucidity'; and for its 'complete avoidance of that technical and turgid terminology which looks scientific, but, for the ordinary reader, is only befogging'. As William Stewart concluded, 'it was for the ordinary reader that the book was written'.[21]

It was certainly written quickly and with a clear purpose in mind. In response to the electoral success of Labour candidates in the general election of 1906, and the transformation of the LRC from a pressure group to a fully-fledged political party, there was substantial public appetite to know more about the new force in British politics. People wanted to find out exactly what it stood for, and – just as importantly – what it had set its face against. As a consequence, George Allen, a mainstream London publisher, commissioned the book from Hardie as part of a series of volumes on the 'Labour Ideal', which was also to include, *Labour and the Empire* by Ramsay MacDonald; *The Woman Socialist* by Ethel Snowden; *The Socialist's Budget* by Philip Snowden; *The Socialist's Church* by Stewart Headlam; and *The Socialist's City* by Fred Jowett. The market for such works was potentially huge. Affiliated unions had brought the LRC just over 353,000 members at its formation, and by 1906-7 its membership was estimated at a million, with all of the major unions now being affiliated to it – with the notable exception of the Miners' Federation, who ran their own candidates separately under the wing of the Liberal Party.

In marked contrast to the Liberal Party – which had been much criticised by the unions for refusing to select working men such as Hardie as Parliamentary candidates – the LRC looked, and thought, like the very people that it sought to represent: 49 of the 50 LRC candidates in the 1906 general election were working men. Ten of them were nominated directly by the ILP, while 32 were nominated by the trade unions, while also being members of the ILP. Furthermore, of the 29 Labour MPs elected to Parliament in January 1906, 23 were active trade unionists, while half had links with religious nonconformity.[22] Among their number were Ramsay MacDonald, who had started out as a pupil-teacher and then as an invoice clerk; Arthur Henderson, an iron moulder and Tyneside trade unionist; Will Crooks, a dockworker who espoused working-class education; and Will Thorne, a former child labourer who had founded the Gasworkers' union. Hardie himself had been a miner before being sacked and blacklisted by the mine owners in Lanarkshire for his trade union activities.

Yet the unions had been won over to the Labour interest not so much through the ideological appeal of Socialism as through the pragmatic need to secure their own survival, which had been threatened by the Taff Vale Judgement of 1901, when the House of Lords had ruled that the Taff Vale Railway Company could claim £23,000 in damages from the railwaymen's union for losses incurred during a recent strike. By means of this judgement the strike – the fundamental weapon of organised labour – had been effectively neutralised through a politically motivated decision by unelected peers. As a consequence, the unions were forced into the political

arena to seek redress through Parliamentary representation, and the newly formed LRC acquired through them a
significance and a level of financial backing that the
earlier Socialist and co-operative groupings had lacked.
This was what enabled it to fight elections more effectively and to pay the salaries of its Members of Parliament.[23]

From the moment that the 29 MPs took their seats in
1906, after the collapse of the Conservative Party at the
ballot box, and the election of a radically orientated
Liberal government with conditional, independent Labour
and trade union support, the LRC was transformed into
an actual Labour Party. Where before there had been
Hardie and two fellow MPs representing the interests of
Labour at Westminster, there was now a recognisable
PLP, with its own organisation, its own programme,
Whips and party leadership. Success, however, had
brought with it new demands, and not a few problems,
the most immediate of which centred about the question
of leadership. Hardie might have been thought of as the
natural choice, but he was only elected as Chairman of
the party by the narrowest of margins – with the backing
of Socialist activists, but in the teeth of concerted opposition from the trade unions. His challenger, David
Shackleton, whose power base lay in the Weavers' union
and who had been elected to Parliament as the result of a
sensational by-election victory in 1902, was essentially a
Liberal. The unions saw in him a more cautious, less
controversial candidate, and a man who possessed a
greater aptitude for administrative and committee work.[24]
In this they were undoubtedly right, and the Labour Party
that emerged after 1906 would owe far more in terms of
its organisation to MacDonald and Henderson than to

Hardie. Yet – somewhat ironically given his posthumous reputation as being a doer rather than a thinker – Hardie was important as a man of ideas, in a way that Shackleton certainly was not. And those ideas were explicitly and consistently Socialist. While many of his new parliamentary colleagues attempted to portray themselves as 'moderate men', and took on the protective colouring, and clubbability, of Westminster, Hardie remained wedded to the idea of the working class, as the only political, economic and cultural dynamo capable of driving through progressive change. He consciously – critics might even say ostentatiously – continued to maintain his stance as a Socialist and outsider. 'Once a man begins to play fast-and-loose with his principles', wrote Hardie, 'he gets on a slippery step, at the bottom of which is the slough of time-serving expediency':

'Easy the descent into Hades', is a saying of which many a good man and woman has lived to experience the bitter meaning. What shall it profit a man though he gains a seat in Parliament and lose his own self-respect?[25]

Having been elected leader of the Labour Party at the age of fifty, Hardie was now – at first sight – at the zenith of his career; he found himself at the helm of an avowedly working-class party that – despite the exclusion from the franchise of women and a sizable percentage of poor, working men – had just triumphed at the polls and had 'begun to realise its possibilities and powers'.[26] Yet, seen from another angle, his powers – as well as those of the fledgling Labour Party – lay far more in their potential, and in the perception of others, than in hard and fast reality on the ground. A life of hardship and unremitting struggle had left Hardie prematurely aged and ill, and the daily business of negotiating parliamentary procedure, juggling the uneasy alliance with the Liberals, and seeking to control faction among his MPs only added to his sense of strain. An opportunity to extend the Eight Hours' Bill to cover the mining industry was somehow missed; and, while Hardie was able to deploy his MPs in order to assist in the passing of reforming legislation on Education, the Licensing of alcohol, and the disestablishment of the Welsh church, progress was not quick enough for his liking on the granting of Home Rule to Ireland. Deep fault-lines also opened up between Liberals and Labour over relief for the unemployed, core economic policy and the future of the House of Lords. The Liberals sought to reform the upper chamber, while Hardie wanted the abolition of the hereditary principle. At the same time, his opposition to Empire – whether British, or foreign – his republicanism, and his support for the growing women's movement and the granting of votes for women, drew censure from a substantial minority on his own benches.

His willingness to work within a broad framework of extra-parliamentary alliances, alongside the PLP, led him to consistently champion the Suffragettes, many of whom were not Socialists or inherently sympathetic to trade unionism, and to offer them space within the pages of *The Labour Leader*. On the one hand this rendered him suspect by those on the more doctrinaire Left; while on the other, the Suffragette tactics of civil disobedience and direct action horrified those on the constitutional, not to say chauvinistic, right.

Westminster left Hardie feeling stifled. He openly declared that 'I feel like a bird with its wings clipped when I am there', and he soon became disillusioned with the priorities and behaviour of many of his colleagues in the PLP.[27] He felt that they lacked zeal, conviction and any real principle, and grumbled that Labour's failings at Westminster stemmed from all those 'luncheons and confabbing with Cabinet Ministers'.[28] In April 1907 his health completely broke down and – temporarily ceding leadership of the party to Shackleton – in May he headed North, to recuperate at a spa that looked out towards the Highlands from the Firth of the Clyde. During his convalescence he conceived of the idea of setting out on a world tour which would, over the course of an eventful year, take in North America, South Africa, Australia, New Zealand and Japan. He would depart in July 1907, setting aside the practical concerns of party building and high politics – and to the horror and disbelief of many of his parliamentary colleagues. However, before leaving, he put the quiet and seclusion of the 'Hydropathic' hotel at Wemyss Bay to good effect, meeting his commitment to George Allen publishers and completing his view of the 'Labour Ideal' – a task that he had seemingly begun at or about the new year – in less than a hundred days.[29] *From Serfdom to Socialism* was written at a whirlwind pace and in 'odd-half hours', and without the recourse to university libraries, and the services of professional researchers, that is the staple of today's politicians and political theorists. It was forged from Hardie's own reading, and from those texts that spoke directly to him and that he valued and loved.

As a consequence, in the pages of his book Carlyle, the Whig historian, sat alongside Kropotkin, the Russian anarchist; the Fabian, Sidney Webb, was quoted beside Karl Marx, the founder of modern Communism; and the Mediaeval Christian doctrine of St Gregory 'the Great' was cited alongside the arguments of William Lecky, the great champion of rationalism and the values of the European Enlightenment. If this heterodoxy has troubled academics, in their collective desire to rigorously pigeon-hole and critique, it was certainly an expression of Hardie's open, auto-didactic and enquiring mind; and it also was reflective of the freedom from dullness and dogma of the Socialist movement in Britain in the first decade of the twentieth century. Hardie's reading of a specifically Socialist canon is hallmarked by creativity and breadth. The harsh industrial, economic, visions of Marx and Belfort Bax co-exist with the rural and Arcadian of Blatchford and Morris; the empiricism and science of Drummond and Darwin with the cheerful paganism, sexual freedoms and eclectic counter-culture advocated by Edward Carpenter. Within the context of a young movement, hesitantly finding its way and estab-lishing an entirely new language, there was much to satisfy both head and heart. Yet, if there was something of Marx there was nothing of Methodism in the mix – contrary to the old canard. Hardie's raw religious impulse, as we shall see later, was rooted in Thomas Muntzer's 'community of goods' rather than in John Wesley's hymn sheets. His engagement with Marx, though located primarily within a reading of the *Communist Manifesto*, was heavily mediated through the more popular, and populist, works of H.M. Hyndman and Belfort Bax. This has led to Hardie being subjected, in the years since his death, to a fair degree of condescension, if not of pure intellectual snobbery. But in Hardie's lifetime Marx tended to be thought of as primarily an economist, and as a revolutionary, rather than as a philosopher (this only changed with the rediscovery and publication of Marx's early texts in the 1960s). Certainly, in 1907, the first volume of *Capital* that was available to Hardie would have conveyed an image of the old economist, mechanistically charting the trajectory and final breakdown of Capitalism, not the youthful editor of the *Neue Rheinische Zeitung* during the 'Year of Revolutions of 1848', or the seasoned author possessed by the radical panoramic vision of the *Grundrisse* (which would remain unpublished until 1939).[30]

What is clear in the book is the influence upon Hardie exerted by Eduard Bernstein and his followers within the Second Socialist International. This is understandable: Bernstein, who lived in London between 1888 and 1901, appeared to have built upon Marx's foundations and to have advanced a highly convincing rationale that accounted for Capitalism's unforeseen adaptability and ability to survive through the dramatic trade depressions of the 1890s and early 1900s. Bernstein also did much to downplay any idea of the immediate, cataclysmic, collapse of Capitalism, or the escalating impoverishment of the working class. His rejection of armed struggle, which had previously been an integral part of Socialist strategy, was also welcome to Hardie and the leaders of the British Labour Party, as was his theorisation of Communist Socialism as an ongoing process rather than as an end point. Similarly, Bernstein's rejection of a rigid economic determinism struck a further chord with Hardie: it appeared to emphasise individual agency and the necessity of organised struggle, rather than the passivity and economic inevitability that was sometimes attributed to Marx by his revisionist bowdlerisers. This said, Hardie's conceptual debt to – and respect for – Marx and his work appears far more strongly in *From Serfdom to Socialism* than was ever acknowledged, or proved comfortable, for his successors in the leadership of the Labour Party (with the possible exceptions of George Lansbury and Michael Foot).

Hardie is in no doubt that the achievement of Socialism was to be 'the next step in the evolution of that form of State which will give the individual the fullest and freest room for expansion and development':

> State Socialism, with all its drawbacks ... will prepare the way for free Communism in which the ... rule of life will be – From each according to his ability, to each according to his needs.[31]

Moreover, though he only quotes directly from Marx on one occasion – and then from the famous injunction of the *Communist Manifesto*, for the workers of all lands to shake off their chains – he frequently paraphrases both him and Engels; and (in a Socialist world as yet undivided and undefined by responses to the October Revolution) he had no difficulty in seeing Communism as encompassing both an original state of grace and the teleology, to which all progressive endeavour must ultimately aspire.[32] Within this context, Hardie sees Marxism as being an organic part of an indigenous radical political tradition that found its fullest expression in the life and career of William Morris – 'the Communist [who] stood lonely and grand like a beacon' on England's shore – and was at the same time the direct heir of both the European Enlightenment and the early Christian Church, inspired by 'the still small voice of Jesus the Communist'.[33]

This understanding permitted him to link the stories and poetry that had inspired him in his youth with the Socialist blueprints offered by the Second International during his manhood. Thus the Highland Clearances, the rising of 1820 and the Scottish Land War of the early 1880s – the history that had shaped him as a radical – came to be understood as part of the history of Capitalism's commodification, its effective privatisation of that which had traditionally been held in common trust. By the time he wrote *From Serfdom to Socialism*, these battles had effectively been brought to a head in both Ireland and Scotland, in the campaign against Landlordism; and it is the parasitical nature of the land-lord, who 'performs no function in the economy of industry or food production', save for the collecting of rents, that moves Hardie to anger. The landlord is simply the agrarian reflection of the industrial capitalist, and his removal 'would pass almost unnoticed' if the land-owning class were to be abolished and the great country estates broken up, since 'the soil and the people who till it would still remain'.[34] For those who think of Hardie as merely reformist, this is hard-edged, inflammatory and truly revolutionary material. The Parliament in which Hardie first sat was still one dominated by the landed interest, and in advocating a major redistribution of wealth from the richest in the land to the very poorest, he was well aware that he was advocating the complete overthrow of the existing political order, rather than its

piecemeal reform. A Parliament stripped of its aristocratic and industrial interest would be a very different
place for Labour representatives to be; and in his conception of the land question, as in other areas, the example
of Parnell's party of Irish MPs – a radical kernel that
forced the pace of Gladstone's Liberals – provided a
model for Hardie's initial conception of the Labour group
at Westminster.

When Hardie thought about the land, he thought
primarily in terms of the struggles of the peasantry of
Ireland and of the Highland crofters of Scotland. His
contact with, and knowledge of, the day labourers
employed in the great estates of England was far more
remote and tangential, and as a consequence the historical passages in *From Serfdom to Socialism* that deal
with the impact of industrialisation upon the English
countryside are by far the weakest and most questionable
in his book. Though the Hammonds' study of *The Village
Labourer* was not to be published for another four years,
Hardie was far too willing to fall back upon overly
romanticised views of the rural and later Mediaeval past,
an interpretation that owed far more to John Ruskin's
imaginative reaction to the spread and sprawl of the
Victorian city than to any reality grounded in the work
of late nineteenth- or early twentieth-century historians.
He telescopes events, over-emphasises the economic and
political freedoms of fifteenth-century peasants and
craftsmen, idealises the welfare provisions offered by the
Monastic orders to the poor and the infirm, and celebrates the pre-Reformation ritual year as symbolising all
that was best in 'Merrie England': plentiful holidays,
maypole dances, cheap food, high wages and 'an eight-

hour day the rule'.[35] The complete absence of political democracy, the domination of the landed aristocracy – as both a warrior and priestly class – the subjugation of women, and the back-breaking nature of a subsistence economy, subject to constant want and the fear of famine, are completely ignored. Even the human cost of the Black Death, which wiped out a third of the population, is skated over by Hardie almost as lightly as it was by Froissart and the courtly chroniclers of the late fourteenth century. In this schema, Hardie's serfs are actually analogous with the women and men under a yet to be realised form of Socialism, while the truly impoverished and downtrodden are the crofters and factory workers of the Industrial Revolution. In this, his desire to make a polemical point threatens to endanger the coherence of his central thesis and to render the stridency of his book's title redundant. Rather than an ascending arc of progress, we are suddenly faced with history as a rather circuitous route, undertaken only in order to recapture something of the glories of the past. This is a world away from the use of history, in the hands of writers like Belfort Bax, as a means of legitimating revolutionary ideas and actions in the present. Yet one wonders if Hardie would have been as quick to abandon his critical faculties, and to accept such a comforting and essentially elitist view of a socially homogeneous Mediaeval past, had he been casting his eyes over the outline of Scottish, as opposed to English, history.

From Serfdom to Socialism is written for a national – British – audience, at a point when English history and culture was held to be dominant over those of the other constituent nations, Scotland, Wales and Ireland. As a consequence, Hardie appears keen to emphasise the work of writers familiar to a primarily English audience; thus he celebrates the pastoral rhapsodies of John Ruskin at the expense of Robbie Burns' grittier hodden hues. But the impact of Burns upon Hardie had been profound and passionately life-changing in a manner that Ruskin's works could never be. Thus, in 1909, Hardie recorded in the pages of *The Labour Leader*:

> I owe more to Robert Burns than to any other man alive or dead. Long ere Carlyle, or Emerson, or Whitman, or Morris had come within my ken ... I had imbibed the liberty-loving spirit and humanitarianism of Burns ... He expressed for me as [a] boy my better self, and gave form and substance to my half-formed thoughts and vague feelings ... His philosophy may not always square with that of the schools, but it never fails to touch the human chord, and therein lies the secret of his power.[36]

It seems therefore that Hardie had sought to rein in his own literary enthusiasms, and to channel them into more readily acceptable, and seemingly more high-brow, forms of expression. His later encapsulation of the Lowland Scot Burns – wrapped in the mantle of the Covenanter Wars and the French Revolution – appears far more compelling and genuine than his tepid appropriation of *Merry England* and the Lakeland poets, which threatens to trivialise the central theme of social justice that runs through the core of *From Serfdom to Socialism*.

However, if Hardie is attempting to force his historical prose to fit the romantic paradigms of others, there

is no doubting the authenticity of his voice and the
distinctive nature of his personal convictions when we
consider his chapter on 'Socialism and Christianity'.
Hardie had consciously come to religion as an adult,
joining the Evangelical Church Union after a conversion
experience, in 1878, 'at the age of about twenty-two'.[37]
Thereafter, he ministered as a lay preacher and a temperance lecturer, who saw the ethical basis for politics best
expressed through Socialism. His conception and practice of religion was intensely personal, and at times
verged upon the mystical, but it was also enacted to a
practical end so as to establish the kingdom of God
here, upon earth. His impetus was rooted in 'the
Christianity of "Christ", as distinct from the
"Christianity" of organised religion, where he found
much hypocrisy', and its inspiration lay in the pages of
Renan's historicised life of Jesus.[38] This attempt to
reclaim the historical 'reality' of Jesus as a man, and
political actor, had an enormous personal appeal for
Hardie. As a result, his pursuit of a religious ideal was
hallmarked by a doctrine of resistance to temporal
powers. The subsequent ossification of Low Church
Protestantism, and its failure to engage with the
Liberation Theology championed by a section of the
Roman Catholic Church in Latin America – as encapsu-
lated in the writings and careers of the Boff brothers,
Dom Helder Camara and Ernesto Cardenale – should
not obscure the revolutionary current that was inherent
in the Protestant Reformation.[39] It was precisely this
strain of religious radicalism – as expressed by John Ball
during the Peasants' Revolt; Jan Hus and Jan Zelivsky
during the Hussite Revolution; and by Thomas Muntzer

at the height of the Peasants' War in Germany – that was being eagerly rediscovered and celebrated across late nineteenth-century Europe by historians and statesmen as different as Frederick Engels, Frantisek Palacky, Belfort Bax and Tomas Masaryk.

As *From Serfdom to Socialism* clearly shows, Keir Hardie was part of this new movement, taking for his heroes Wycliffe and Ball, Muntzer and Winstanley, and emphasising their 'Communistic teachings', and rooted in a belief 'that Communism in goods was practised by Christians for at least three hundred three hundred years after the death of Christ'.[40] For Hardie, the Sermon on the Mount was far more radical, and went 'far in advance of' anything 'ever put forward by any Communist, ancient or modern': 'Christ's denunciations of wealth are only equalled by the fierceness of the diatribes which He levelled against the Pharisees'.[41] This is not the nebulous recourse to the doctrinal morality of the established churches, repackaged as 'Christian Socialism', that we have seen in more recent leaders of the Labour Party – more at home, one suspects, taking tea with the Reverend Slope at Barchester Towers than marching alongside the Covenanter rebels at Drumclog and Airds Moss. Rather, it is a theory of social and religious liberation, based upon a conception of a historical Jesus who threw the money lenders out of the Temple at Jerusalem. All of a sudden, the platitudes used to deaden Hardie's radicalism through the prism of his Christian beliefs appear to be spectacularly misplaced. His sense of a personal god, become man, made him more revolutionary – as both theologian and politician – than would ever otherwise have been the case. Thus, as he reminds his audience:

The respectable, church-going men who are, without cause, raising the price of coal in the depth of winter, and raising it most against the poor, are worse than common cheats and robbers. They are robbing the poor, not merely of money, but of comfort, of health and, in some cases, of life. They are worse criminals than the cut-throat and burglar. You have a chance to protect yourself against these, but you cannot escape the others. They may attend church or chapel regularly; they may be respected members of society ... but they are robbers all the same.[42]

If Hardie was a religious radical, then he was also a polemicist on behalf of radical feminism. His engagement with women's rights was both long-standing and heartfelt. A volume dealing specifically with *The Woman Socialist* had already been commissioned from Ethel Snowden for the 'Labour Ideal' series, but, as with Christianity, Hardie felt impelled to emphasise that this was not tangential to, but an integral and non-negotiable part of, his conception of Socialism. Initially influenced by August Bebel's exposition of *Woman Under Socialism*, Hardie then came into the political and personal orbit of Emmeline Pankhurst, and her daughters Christabel and Sylvia. His leadership had ensured that Labour was the only party in Parliament committed to women's suffrage, and that it had moved to introduce its own Women's Enfranchisement Bill at Westminster, in 1907. As Kenneth O. Morgan perceptively highlighted: 'No other Labour member championed the women's cause in so uninhibited and uncompromising manner as did Hardie'.[43] He spoke out in Parliament after suffragette demonstrations were broken up by the police in Trafalgar Square, raised questions about the convictions and treatment of women activists imprisoned in Holloway jail, and advocated the opening of crèches at workplaces. And while he was leading the new Labour Party at Westminster, he was also committing more and more of his time to promoting women's suffrage. It was quite clear in his own mind that the cause of women and the cause of Socialism were one and the same. The trouble was that neither the suffragettes themselves, nor many within the ranks of his own party, shared the same confidence. The outlook and composition of the Pankhurst's WSPU (the Women's Social and Political Union) was firmly middle- as opposed to working-class, and at the Cockermouth by-election in the summer of 1906 Emmeline Pankhurst chose to attack the Liberal candidate for opposing women's suffrage, while refraining from endorsing his Labour rival. The result of this decision, made on the grounds of 'rising above' party politics, was to help the Conservative candidate on his way to victory. This neatly consolidated the politically and socially conservative wing of the WSPU under the Pankhursts' control, but it left Hardie's policy of unconditional support for the suffragettes dangerously exposed, and provoked widespread rage among the membership of the Labour Party, which understandably felt that it had been betrayed by its allies. The hostile image of the suffragettes as snobbish dilettantes, who cared little for their working-class sisters and nothing at all for the campaign for votes for poor men, seemed to have been confirmed. Margaret Bondfield, who sat as one of the three women on the Executive of the ILP, noted that 'what women required was not votes, but industrial organisation', and characterised the WSPU as being 'the hobby horse of disappointed old maids whom no one had wanted to marry'.[44] Hardie had come to expect such comments from some of his male trade union colleagues, but to find them echoed by a prominent woman activist, who had risen from the shop floor – and who would continue to rise, becoming the first woman cabinet minister in 1929 – was both troubling and utterly perplexing. Worse was to come, as Hardie's attempt to force through legislation in line with the WSPU programme met with a storm of opposition from inside his own party, at Labour's 1907 conference. Bondfield, who a year earlier had founded the WLL (the Women's Labour League) in opposition to the Pankhursts' organisation, led calls for Labour to re-orientate its policy to focus upon universal suffrage, regardless of either gender or property qualifications. Hardie's authority could not but suffer, and, though he eventually swung an unwilling party behind his position, it was a pyrrhic victory. The battle contributed to the breaking of his health, and the onset of the minor stroke that sent him to take the waters at Wemyss Bay.

As William Stewart appreciated, the question of votes for women was a poisoned chalice, which contained potentially 'disintegrating' properties for the fledgling Labour Party; and with this in mind it is noticeable that Hardie is inclined to be somewhat vague in the pages of *From Serfdom to Socialism* over precisely how the vote is to be obtained and how women are to be truly emancipated under Socialism. In the main, he reprises Bebel's ideas – though steering clear of his more Bohemian arguments about the drawbacks of marriage and the beneficial nature of free love – arguing that through Socialism 'the sexes shall meet on terms of freedom and equality'.[45] As the Capitalist system was intrinsically governed by 'strength and brutality', it followed that 'the gentle and the weak' must be subordinated and 'go to the wall', with womankind becoming 'economically dependent upon man'.[46] Elsewhere, Hardie is on less sure ground, oscillating wildly between the theories of eugenicists such as Karl Pearson, Marxists of the stamp of Karl Kautsky and classical economists like John Stuart Mill, in order to suggest that the 'position of women would ... be revolutionised by Socialism'. Though his arguments in favour of feminism are far less sophisticated than those advanced by his friend and comrade James Connolly, Hardie is still able to make his case for the political desirability, and moral necessity, of gender equality in a way that goes far beyond the attainment of the right to vote.[47] 'Under Socialism', he concludes:

> when the woman, whether as wife, mother or worker, will have a claim in her own right to a share in the national wealth, she will at once emerge into greater freedom. In choosing a mate she will no longer be driven by hard economic necessity to accept the most eligible offer from the worldly point of view, but will be guided exclusively by all-compelling love and the need for congenial companionship.[48]

If at times within the structure of *From Serfdom to Socialism* Hardie seems committed to outlining the contours of his future utopias, he is also prepared to examine the well-springs of Labour's electoral power. He took local government very seriously, and understood full well that at that time the real strength of the Labour Party lay in the town halls rather than in the Palace of Westminster. After the Second Great Reform Act of 1867 had enfranchised a segment of the male working class, candidates from relatively modest backgrounds had begun to make their mark in local politics – initially as Liberals or Progressives, and later as Socialists. Working men were first elected to the School Boards created as a result of the Education Reform Act of 1870, and then to the local councils. They began to rapidly erode the Liberal power bases in the municipalities, to the extent that, despite its continued success as a party of national government right up until 1914, the hold of the Liberals upon the organs of grassroots democracy had long since been wrested away by Labour. London, which became a County Council in 1889, was the key to Labour's success, and an enduring reservoir of support during times of difficulty and dissention. It is not therefore surprising to discover that Keir Hardie's triumphant break-through in the general election of 1892, which saw him returned as the very first Labour MP, was built upon years of patient work by Socialists and trades unionists to secure control of the local government of West Ham. At the time of the 1906 general election there were only 56 Labour councillors spread across the British Isles, but by 1913 this figure had risen to 184; while the number of trades councils and local Labour parties affiliated to the national party rose from just 73 in 1905-6, to 177 in 1914.[49] As Hardie pithily observed: 'What the Capitalist class fears is not neurotic shouting, but steady, plodding, under-mining work, which will bring the whole structure about their heads'.[50] It was small wonder, then, that he should see fit to devote a whole chapter of *From Serfdom to Socialism* to the theme of government from the grassroots-up, or that, given that 'property held and worked and controlled by the municipalities already exceeds £500,000,000 sterling in value and is being added to yearly', he could think that: 'This process has but to continue long enough to ensure that every industry will pass under public control, and thus State Socialism will become an accomplished fact'.[51]

Within this framework, there was no sense of the gradual withering away of the state; rather, the bastions of Capitalism would begin to tumble one by one before the electoral tsunami harnessed by Socialism, permitting the levers of state power to be delivered, intact and by means 'of easy transition', to an incoming Socialist government. Now, this deceptively simple formula negates all of the problems of revolutionary transition that have preoccupied political theorists from Jefferson to Lenin, and from Gramsci to Negri and Hardt, and is as close to economic determinism as Hardie ever came. However, elsewhere, as we shall see, he suggests something quite different. *From Serfdom to Socialism* appears to have been written in conscious tension between the need to convince the trade union leadership of the benefits and practicalities of Socialism, the desire to express Hardie's own vision, and the sure knowledge that the movement's left wing, rooted in Hyndman's SDF, had gone into self-imposed exile in the pursuit of doctrinal rigour. Consequently, though Hardie recognises that 'the modern State exists primarily to protect property, and will destroy life as freely as it is destroyed either in the caverns of the ocean or the depths of the forest rather than allow property to be forcibly interfered with in the slightest degree', he refrains from the obvious conclusion that it will, therefore, be prepared to fight to the death in order to preserve its ill-gotten gains.[52] He skates around what is uncomfortable, until such time as his own supporters have signed up to his basic premise, hoping that the details will be worked out in the fullness of time. Thus, Hardie seeks to turn vacuum to virtue, celebrating the lack of a programme as an absence of dogma, and putting to good use the considerable flexibility that this afforded him; confiding that the desire to outline 'the form the Socialist State shall take is to play the fool', for: 'That belongs to the future, and is a matter with which posterity alone can deal'.[53]

This said, if his writings are shot through with a sense of romanticism and a sense of what is left unsaid, they are also punctuated with a steely realism: if there were to be roses, there must first be bread. The posthumous image of the unworldly Hardie – part seer, part poet – does him an injustice and detracts from his acumen, the scope of his ambitions and his will to succeed, whatever the odds stacked against him. He was far from guileless, as his critics, not least of whom would number Henry Hyndman and John Burns, would discover to their cost: 'under an appearance of simple rugged honesty he concealed much subtlety in compassing their defeat'.[54] Moreover, he knew for what he fought, the nature of the vested interests that he challenged, and the price he would have to pay in waging that battle. 'No reform worthy of the name', he wrote, 'can come to the Working Class which does not

poach on the preserves of some privileged class'.[55] Change
would not, after all, come without a fight.

Without this element of toughness, born out of principle and a large measure of self-belief, he would simply
have been swallowed up on the Liberal benches after
1892, tamed by the Parliamentary system, and silenced
not through persecution but by flattery and comfort.
That this did not happen, as had been confidently
predicted by his establishment critics, and that he
preserved the distinctiveness of his Socialist voice amid
the privileged chatter of Westminster, would seem to
confirm the verdict of John Bruce Glasier, writing in
direct response to the anodyne speech that was delivered
over his coffin in 1915. Hardie was, he thought 'unprec-
edented as a working-class leader in our country':

> He was the first man from the midst of the working
> class who completely understood them, completely
> sympathised with them, completely championed
> them. He was the first working man who, having
> entered Parliament, never deserted them, never turned
> his back on a single principle which he had professed,
> never drifted away from his class in thought, in feeling
> or in faith. When he came there was no Labour repre-
> sentation in our country. The Trade Union movement
> was in feudal knights' Fee to the Liberal Party. The
> Working Class had no political mind of their own.
> Parliament was no more theirs than was the work-
> shop or the factory. Their masters ruled in both.[56]

This is not suggestive of mere gesture politics, nor of the
air of profound failure that has often been used to shroud

his career. It is a useful convention to seek to portray anyone who struggles for radical change to free-market Capitalism as being a blood-crazed fanatic – see Robespierre; a harmless crank – see Carpenter; or as a doomed and impractical martyr, as has been the case with Hardie. In each example, the message is that the battle is a futile one and that the end result is likely to be far worse than the original sickness. It limits horizons, closes off debates and effectively dehumanises or trivialises divergent voices. Furthermore, the sense of futility that such projections have embedded within the victims, and potential critics, of Capitalism has done much to confirm the intellectual and economic triumph of neoliberalism, and to destroy the self confidence and pride of the British Labour Movement. If you are unaware of the scope of the achievements of the past, and prepared to accept received wisdoms rather than to discover the course of an argument for yourself, then the status quo will go forever unchallenged, and the myth establishes itself as inviolable fact.

This returns us to our initial contention regarding the importance of *From Serfdom to Socialism*. It was conceived of as a testament to principle, written to satisfy a highly diverse alliance of labour interests – a heterogeneous federation of Socialists, co-operators and trades unionists – and sought to convey to them a coherent platform for Socialism, and a vision of what they could hope to achieve through their collective efforts. It was conditioned by Hardie's guiding aims to create a mass movement that looked outwards, rather than inwards, and 'to persuade, propagandise and permeate' first the trade unions themselves, and then the wider working class, with the merits of Socialism.[57] It could comprehend an Edward

Carpenter as well as an Ernest Bevin. To this end, there were to be no doctrinal proscriptions or expulsions under Hardie's Labour Party, and, if it existed for the working class, it would also welcome middle-class, or even aristocratic supporters. As Hardie explained in 1888: 'If ... anyone, peasant or peer, is found willing to accept the programme and work with the party, his help will be gladly accepted'.[58] As a consequence, Hardie designed his Labour Party in order to expand, to include, and not to alienate. It was meant to be amorphous and indistinct, all those things that infuriate political historians and theorists, but which actually proved in the long term to be the very strengths which enabled Labour to emerge, after 1918, as the foremost Social Democratic party not just in Europe but in the world. The prime function of the Labour Party, as Hardie saw it, was to unite working people, politically; and this is precisely what he achieved. It was in this context that James Maxton thought that Hardie had finally transcended the label of 'agitator' to become both prophet and pioneer, for: 'He made vocal the desires and aspirations of the men and women of the working class of his time, and taught them how to express them collectively for themselves'.[59] The Lanarkshire Miner who felt possessed by a mission 'to stir up a divine discontent with wrong' had forged *From Serfdom to Socialism* in order to shape the growth of a new party, founded upon fraternity and justice, and to revolutionise and to transform the whole of British society.[60] In so doing, he kept faith with himself and maintained his essential credo that had 'no sympathy whatever with a system which robs the nation of its wealth, acts as a drag on industry, and cheats labour of its own':

I would cordially support all forms of legislation which would rid honest industry of the useless idler, whether personified in the absentee landlord, the sweating shareholder, or the gambling and swindling stockbroker. My first concern is the moral and material well-being of the working classes, and ... I will in every case place the claims of Labour above those of Party. I reserve to myself the absolute and unconditional right to take such action, irrespective of the exigencies of Party welfare, as may seem to be needful in the interest of the workers.[61]

Happy and fulfilled can be the woman, or man, who can achieve more or say fairer than that.

John Callow, 17 April 2015

NOTES

1. Hardie quoted in: H. Fyfe, *Keir Hardie*, Duckworth, London 1935, p139.
2. J. Joll, *The Second International, 1889-1914*, Harper Colophon Books, New York 1966, pp173-184; & C. MacKie, *Dedicated to the Memory of James Keir Hardie MP*, self-published, Kilmarnock 1916, p1.
3. F. Brockway, *The Keir Hardie I Knew,* intro. N. Kinnock, Hyde Park Pamphlet no.10, L.S.A. Jones, self-published, London 1987, p5.
4. See the account of Hardie's funeral in Caroline Benn's seminal biography: C. Benn, *Keir Hardie*, Richard Cohen Books, London 1992, rpt. 1997, pp351-352.
5. J. Cockburn, *The Hungry Heart. A Romantic Biography of James Keir Hardie*, Jarrolds Ltd, London 1956.
6. See: *Brass*, ITV, 1983-84, released on DVD by Network films in 2007.

7. G.D.H. Cole, *James Keir Hardie*, Fabian Society/Victor Gollancz Ltd, London 1941, p5; & H.N. Brailsford, *The Memory of Hardie*, ILP, London, n/d c.1915, pp2-3.

8. Viscount Samuel, W. Elliott, H. Gaitskell & W.S. Morrison, *Keir Hardie and the House of Commons*, intro. F. Brockway, Keir Hardie Memorial Committee, London 1956, p7; & H.N. Brailsford, *The Memory of Hardie*, ILP, London n/d c.1915, pp2-3.

9. Labour Party, *James Keir Hardie. Pioneer Socialist. Centenary Celebrations*, Labour Party, Scottish Council, Glasgow 1956, p5.

10. See: H. MacNicol, Pioneer Theatre in association with Moral Re-Armament, *Keir Hardie – The Man they Couldn't Buy*, Pioneer Theatre in association with Moral Re-Armament, no place 1980; & Pioneer Theatre in association with Moral Re-Armament, *What's Missing in Politics Today?*, Birmingham, November 1979. Strangely, for a play about an anti-imperialist, a large proportion of the cast came from the former colonial and business administration of Southern Africa, and had had commercial interests in Zambia.

11. F. Brockway, *The Keir Hardie I Knew*, intro. N. Kinnock, Hyde Park Pamphlet no.10, L.S.A. Jones, self-published, London, 1987, p1.

12. T. Wright & M. Carter, *The People's Party. The History of the Labour Party*, intro. T. Blair, Thames & Hudson, London 1997, p7.

13. Hardie barely rates ten mentions in 187 pages of text, and Macdonald's writings rather than Hardie's are those that are quoted as marking the foundations of the Labour Party.

14. Wright & Carter, *The People's Party*, pp19 & 27. A more recent history of the party is similarly dismissive: see M. Pugh, *Speak for Britain! A New History of the Labour Party*, Vintage Books, London 2011, pp24-25. When compared with the seminal role accorded to Hardie, just a few years previously, in A.J. Davies' history of the Labour Party, the difference and decline in perceptions of his importance is dramatic and very marked. See A.J. Davies, *To Build a New Jerusalem. The British Labour Party from Keir Hardie to Tony Blair*, Abacus, London 1992, rpt. 1996, pp17-50.

15. See: R. Leonard, 'A Prophet in his Land. Why the Legacy of Socialist Titan James Keir Hardie must be Remembered', *Morning Star*, 3 January 2008, p7.

16. See: R. Miliband, *Parliamentary Socialism: A Study in the Politics of Labour*, Merlin Press Ltd., London 1964, rpt. 2009, passim, for a withering critique of 'Labourism'.

17. I. McLean, *Keir Hardie*, Allen Lane, London 1975, p172; & R.E. Dowse, edited & intro., *From Serfdom to Socialism, by James Keir Hardie; Labour and the Empire, by James Ramsay MacDonald; The Socialist Budget by Philip Snowden*, The Harvester Press, Hassocks nr. Brighton 1974, pp viii-ix, xiii, xv, xviii-xxi, xxiv & xxx-xxxi. The chorus of opprobrium seems even to have coloured Caroline Benn's response to *Serfdom to Socialism*, as she uncharacteristically labelled the book as a mere 'essay', resembling 'a long Whitmanesque prose poem, and [which] might be read as such'. Kenneth Morgan took a more measured view, seeing Hardie's major full-length work as 'an honest attempt, by a man with little formal education, to work out a personal position' on Socialism. See: C. Benn, *Keir Hardie*, Richard Cohen Books, London 1997, p244; & K. O. Morgan, *Keir Hardie, Radical and Socialist*, Weidenfeld & Nicolson, London 1975, p202.

18. Dowse (ed. & intro), *From Serfdom to Socialism*, pp x & xxiv.

19. Dowse (ed. & intro), *From Serfdom to Socialism*, pp xx-xi.

20. E. Hughes (ed.), *Keir Hardie's Speeches and Writings (From 1888 to 1915)*, Forward Printing & Publishing, Glasgow, n/d but 1928, pp12-13, 38-39, 45-47, 79-80, 93-102, 126-128, 129-135 & 142-148; & J. Keir Hardie, *India, Impressions and Suggestions*, ILP, London 1909, passim.

21. W. Stewart, *J. Keir Hardie. A Biography*, intro. J. R. MacDonald, ILP/Keir Hardie Memorial Fund, London 1921, p240.

22. Davies, *To Build a New Jerusalem*, p40.

23. K.D. Brown (ed.), *The First Labour Party, 1906-1914*, Croom Helm, London, Sydney, New Hampshire 1985, pp113 & 147: R. Moore, *The Emergence of the Labour Party*, Hodder & Stoughton, London 1978, pp81, 87-89 & 91-92.

24. Benn, *Keir Hardie*, pp208-209; Moore, *Emergence of the Labour Party*, pp103-104; & K.O. Morgan, *Keir Hardie: Radical and Socialist*, Weidenfeld & Nicolson, London, 1975, pp154-155.

25. Hardie quoted in: Fyfe, *Keir Hardie*, p115.

26. E. Smith, *From Pit to Parliament: Keir Hardie's Life Story*, The People's Press, Stockport 1909, p11.

27. Hardie quoted in: Davies, *To Build a New Jerusalem*, p35.

28. Hardie quoted in: Morgan, *Keir Hardie*, p172.

29. Stewart, *Keir Hardie*, pp245-247. The timescale for the writing of the book is far from clear. Hardie dates his foreword as being composed on New Year's Day 1907; but there is evidence presented by his recent biographers that he used his time recuperating on the coast of the Clyde to complete the bulk of the writing. See: Benn, *Keir Hardie*, p228; & Morgan, *Keir Hardie*, p205.

30. It would seem that Hardie used the following edition of Marx: K. Marx, *Capital: A Critical Analysis of Capitalist Production*, Swan Sonnenschien & Co., London, 1902.

31. See this volume: J. Keir Hardie, *From Serfdom to Socialism*, intro. J. Callow, Lawrence & Wishart, London 2015, p27.

32. Hardie, *From Serfdom to Socialism*, 2015, p125.

33. Hardie, *From Serfdom to Socialism*, 2015, p123.

34. Hardie, *From Serfdom to Socialism*, 2015, p28.

35. J. L. & B. Hammond, *The Village Labourer, 1760-1832. A Study in the Government of England before the Reform Bill*, Longmans, Green & Co., London, New York, Bombay & Calcutta 1911; & Hardie, *From Serfdom to Socialism*, 2015, pp45-48 & 51.

36. Keir Hardie, *The Labour Leader*, 22 January 1909, quoted in: Hughes (ed.), *Keir Hardie's Speeches and Writings*, p139.

37. Keir Hardie quoted in: Cole, *James Keir Hardie*, p19; A.J. Forson, *A Tribute to the late J. Keir Hardie MP*, Civic Press, no place or date, c.1915, p2; & Johnson, *Keir Hardie's Socialism*, p4.

38. G. Lean, *Keir Hardie. Father of the British Labour Movement*, The Waterfront & Industrial Pioneer, Birmingham, n/d, c.1979-80, p17; & E. Renan, *Life of Jesus*, Carleton & Michel Levy, New York & Paris 1864.

39. For Liberation Theology, see: G. Gutierrez, *A Theology of*

Liberation. History, Politics and Salvation, trans. & ed. C. Inda & J. Eagleson, SCM Press Ltd., London 1974.

40. Hardie, *From Serfdom to Socialism*, 2015, p33.
41. Hardie, *From Serfdom to Socialism*, 2015, p33.
42. Hardie quoted in: Fyfe, *Keir Hardie*, pp121-122.
43. Morgan, *Keir Hardie*, p167; & A. Bebel, *Woman under Socialism*, trans. D. De Leon, New York Labor News Company, New York 1904.
44. Margaret Bondfield quoted in: Benn, *Keir Hardie*, p199.
45. Hardie, *From Serfdom to Socialism*, 2015, p37.
46. Hardie, *From Serfdom to Socialism*, 2015, p37.
47. D. Nevin (ed.), *Writings of James Connolly – Political Writings, 1893-1916*, SIPTU, Dublin, 2011, pp54-55, 62-63; & J. Connolly, *Selected Writings*, ed. & intro. P. Berresford Ellis, Monthly Review Press, New York & London, 1973, pp189-195.
48. Hardie, *From Serfdom to Socialism*, 2015, p108.
49. E. Royle, *Modern Britain. A Social History, 1750-1985*, Edward Arnold, London & New York, 1987 rpt. 1989, p142.
50. Hardie quoted in: Fyfe, *Keir Hardie*, p127.
51. Hardie, *From Serfdom to Socialism*, 2015, p74.
52. Hardie, *From Serfdom to Socialism*, 2015, p39–40.
53. Hardie quoted in: Johnson, *Keir Hardie's Socialism*, p8.
54. Cole, *James Keir Hardie*, p33.
55. Johnson, *Keir Hardie's Socialism*, p5.
56. J. Bruce Glasier quoted in: Anon., *Presentation and Unveiling of Bust of Keir Hardie (MP for West Ham South, 1892-95), at the West Ham Town Hall, Stratford, E15, Tuesday 20th January 1948*, National Labour Press, London 1948, p4.
57. Morgan, *Keir Hardie*, p211.
58. Hardie quoted in: Davies, *To Build a New Jerusalem*, p27.
59. J. Maxton, *Keir Hardie. Prophet and Pioneer*, Francis Johnson, n/d but 1939, p15.
60. Keir Hardie quoted in: Maxton, *Keir Hardie. Prophet and Pioneer*, p14.
61. Keir Hardie quoted in: Anon., *Presentation and Unveiling of Bust of Keir Hardie*, p2.

FOREWORD

THE ATTITUDE OF multitudes of people towards Socialism is that of the man who could not see the wood for the trees. They are so engrossed in the contemplation of petty details that they never get even a remote glimpse of the great unifying principle underlying Socialism. Who is to blacken the boots and do the scavenging? What about the dangerous and disagreeable occupations such as mining and seafaring? How are we going to secure that each does his fair share and no more of the work, and receive his fair share and no more of the resultant wealth? How is genius to be rewarded under Socialism, and how is Art to be recognised? Since all are to be equal, what is to become of the man with exceptional ability? Is he to be specially rewarded? If not, what incentive will there be to his putting forth his special abilities, and if he is, what becomes of the promised equality?

These and a hundred and one others of a like kind are the objections with which the Socialist advocate is continually being met. Unless he can give a detailed and circumstantial explanation of how each and every one of these difficulties is to be overcome, his opponent goes away exulting in the belief that he has demolished the case for Socialism. With great respect I venture to submit that none of these things at all affect the question at issue, which is whether Socialism represents a desirable set of principles which, if acted upon, would materially lessen the burden of human woe and tend to the further development and improvement of the human race. If it be admitted that such results would follow the adoption of Socialism, then the adaptation of means to realise that end should present but few, and those easily overcome, difficulties. It is only by leaving out all allowance for common sense that the difficulties appear to be great and insuperable.

It is not within the scope of my intention in writing this little brochure to enter into an elaborate disquisition on the historical basis of Socialism, or to embody its economic theories and principles in a learned treatise. These things have been done by other and more competent hands. The moving Why which guides me is the belief I have of the need there is of a brief unadorned statement of the case for Socialism, easily understandable by plain folk, and in which incidentally some of the objections of our opponents may be met and some of the difficulties in the way of the earnest seeker after truth may be removed. It has been written, literally, in the odd half-hours of a busy period in a life crowded with work. Whilst I have sought to buttress my opinions by quotations from writers of recognised authority, I do not in any way seek to shelter myself behind them.

For the opinions expressed I hold myself alone responsible, and desire it to be clearly understood that no one
else is committed by them. I have provided a list of
works at the end of the book which may be read by
those who desire to learn more about Socialism and
the issues which it raises.

J. K. H.
1st January 1907.

CHAPTER 1

BASIC PRINCIPLES

S OCIALISM IS MUCH more than either a political creed or an economic dogma. It presents to the modern world a new conception of society and a new basis upon which to build up the life of the individual and of the State. Hitherto we have been accustomed to assume that because in the lower phases of life we witness what appears to be a continual struggle for existence, with the barriers of want ever pressing against the increasing multitudes of animals and plants requiring support, that these same conditions must also necessarily apply to human existence. Nature red in tooth and claw, may be a faithful description of the conditions which accompany the struggle for life in the depth of the jungle – although even this is now open to grave doubt – but, admitting for the moment for the sake of argument that such is the case, that does not seem to give any justification for reason-endowed man allowing himself to be guided in his organisation of society by the laws which govern the life of the unreasoning brute. For what purpose has man been endowed with reason if not to enable him to rise above the brute creation, not merely in his organisation of the means of procuring food, but also in the relation of the individual towards his fellows? If the law of the jungle is to be his rule of life, what becomes of his claim to be a religious being endowed with an immortal soul?

To the Socialist the community represents a huge family organisation in which the strong should employ their gifts in promoting the weal of all, instead of using their strength for their own personal aggrandisement. In like manner the community of States which compose the world, and making full allowance for the differences of environment, of tradition, and of evolution, he regards as a great comity which should be co-operating for the elevation of the race. Believing these things, the Socialists of all lands are working for their realisation. Herbert Spencer has pointed out that Altruism – each for all and all for each – is but the highest form of enlightened selfishness. He and the school of Individualists to which he belonged, and which still has its representatives, although a dwindling band, differed from the Socialist only in the method by which he sought to achieve the end which both have in common, the freedom of the individual. To Spencer any interference with the freedom of individual action seemed baneful. He conceived society as a collection of units, each one struggling to make the best of his individual life and thus finding the niche in life which he was intended to occupy, whilst learning by experience that co-operation and not competition is the only true basis upon which progress can be built. But the cooperation must be free and voluntary, and not imposed from without by any law other than that of enlightened self-interest. This conception of the evolution of society has great attractions, but it presupposes certain conditions which do not exist. The judge, the soldier, and the policeman are violations of the basic law upon which Spencer founded his thesis. Restraint is restraint whether it be a Factory Act or a Peace Preservation Act, and if the State has no right to interfere to protect the poor struggling against circumstances over which they have no control in the industrial world, it is difficult to see why the same State should be considered a beneficent agency when called in to protect the property of the rich against an infuriated mob of starving people. If the poor are to be left to struggle for existence unaided by the State, then why not the rich? If it be replied that the State is part of the environment which the owners of property have evolved for their own protection, the obvious answer is that so soon as the working-class succeed in capturing and controlling the machinery of the State it will then also become part of their natural environment. The law of evolution leaves no doubt on the point, that there comes a time when the individual, unable to struggle longer against overwhelming odds, succumbs, and that whole species have thus disappeared from the animal and vegetable worlds. It is no reply in this connection to say that higher forms of life have taken their place. If it could be shown that the great Trust magnate or the great Aristocratic landowner, apart from the advantages of his inherited wealth, was a more highly developed species of humanity than the poor struggling sempstress or the unemployed docker, then there might be some justification for allowing the docker and the sempstress as the representatives of a weaker class to die out in order to enable the more highly developed creature to survive; but one moment's reflection will show that the alleged superiority of the landowner or the Trust magnate rests on one fact alone, namely, that he owns certain material possessions, usually inherited, which enable him to dictate the terms upon which his less fortunate fellow-creatures shall be permitted to live. And really in the end he is more dependent upon them than they on him. Were they to die out, he also would die with them, he being but a parasite whose life is dependent upon their continued existence; whereas, his disappearance as a class would free the other classes from a great weight with which they are now burdened, and thus leave them much better equipped for the battle of life. If, then, all men are to be free, in the Individualistic sense of that term, then an indispensable preliminary is the abolition of the State and the free grouping together of sections of the community according to their respective affinities. Men like Tolstoy and Kropotkin openly advocate a revolutionary change of this kind, and in this they are at least consistent. When brought face to face with the probable outcome of their own theories, however, they admit that in place of the State there would grow up great Co-operative organisations, and that these would require to work together for mutual aid and support, and would necessarily require rules and regulations for their guidance, so that in the end we should get back to pretty much the existing organisation, only under another guise. The State as we know it is a growth born of the needs of the times, and is continually adapting itself to meet the changing influence which controls its working. The assumption that under the voluntary Cooperative organisation plan each individual would be free either to submit or not as he pleased to the will of the majority, is a pure fallacy. Under the State now each individual is free to act as he pleases provided he is willing to take the consequences. Hunger is a much more potent weapon than any form of penal enactment for bringing an insubordinate member of the community to subjection, and under any conceivable form of voluntary cooperation the individual who put himself in opposition to the clearly expressed will of his fellows would fare no better than he does at present. The individualistic conception of the State as some external authority exercising a malign influence upon the life of the community is a travesty of fact. The State is that form of organised society which has evolved through the process of the ages, and represents the aptitude for freedom and self-government to which any people has attained. The policeman and the soldier, for example, who are at the call of the landlord or the employer when tenant or workman becomes turbulent, exist by the will and under the express authority of those same tenants and workmen, who constitute a preponderating majority in the State, and without whose consent neither soldier nor policeman could continue to exist. It is their toil which pays for their maintenance; it is from their ranks that they are drawn; and it is their votes which create the Parliament which creates the policeman and the soldier. The Socialist therefore, recognising that the State is but the expression of the will of the people, accepts it as an existing fact, and seeks by means of the education of the electorate to change the conception upon which the State at present rests and the functions which it exercises. Theoretically, the State exists to protect life and property: in fact, the modern State exists primarily to protect property, and will destroy life as freely as it is destroyed either in the caverns of the ocean or the depths of the forest rather than allow property to be forcibly interfered with in the slightest degree. This, however, is but natural when we remember that in the past only the propertied classes had any real influence in the moulding of the State. From the dawn of history we get glimpses of the toiling multitude slowly emerging from serfdom. We see one section after another painfully winning its way into political recognition, but always as the owners of property. Hence the fact that the State is primarily concerned with the preservation of the rights of property. The aristocrat as the great war lord, the yeoman as his captain, the trading and commercial classes, and the great barons of finance have all in turn succeeded in asserting themselves and impressing their will upon the State. As each of these sections have won recognition for themselves they have recognised that they had a common interest with all the rest in keeping the propertyless mass of the common people in subjection, and have joined forces for that purpose. Obviously the surest method for keeping the masses in subjection to their lords in the olden time was to make the land private property. A landless peasantry could have no rights.

Latter years have seen the Capitalist and Commercial classes successfully winning their way to influence and power in the councils of the nation, and they in turn have surrounded their particular form of property – Capital – with the odour of sanctity and reduced the artisan to the same dependent position as the landless peasant. No law can give freedom to a people which is dependent upon some power or authority outside themselves for the necessaries of life. The owners of the means of life can dictate the terms upon which all who are not owners are to be permitted to live. This is the great new fact which Socialists are bringing to the front. Socialism says to the worker, It is not the State which holds you in bondage, it is the private monopoly of those means of life without which you cannot live, and until you make these means of life the common property and inheritance of all you can never hope to escape from your bondage. The economic object of Socialism, therefore, is to make land and industrial capital common property, and to cease to produce for the profit of the landlord and the capitalist and to begin to produce for the use of the community.

The disinherited and propertyless people are learning that Socialism and freedom "gang thegither," and will use the State as the means whereby property, and the freedom which its possession ensures, shall become the common inheritance of every citizen.

This change in the ownership of land and capital and in the object of production, however, is merely the medium through which it is hoped the Socialist spirit will find expression. Socialism implies the inherent equality of all human beings. It does not assume that all are alike, but only that all are equal. Holding this to be true of individuals, the Socialist applies it also to races. Only by a full and unqualified recognition of this claim can peace be restored to the world. Socialism implies brotherhood, and brotherhood implies a living recognition of the fact that the duty of the strong is not to hold the weak in subjection, but to assist them to rise higher and ever higher in the scale of humanity, and that this cannot be done by trampling upon and exploiting their weakness but by caring for them and showing them the better way.

CHAPTER 2

MUNICIPAL SOCIALISM

S OCIALISM DOES NOT propose to abolish land or capital. Only a genius could have thought of this as an objection to Socialism. Socialism proposes to abolish capitalism and landlordism. The landlord, *qua* landlord, performs no function in the economy of industry or of food production. He is a rent receiver; that, and nothing more. Were the landlord to be abolished, the soil and the people who till it would still remain, and the disappearance of the landowner would pass almost unnoticed. So too with the capitalist. I do not refer to the man who manages his own business; he is a business manager, not a capitalist. By capitalist, I mean the investor who puts his money into a concern and draws profits therefrom without participating in the organisation or management of the business. Were all these to disappear in the night, leaving no trace behind, nothing would be changed. The capital would remain; the engineers, architects, organisers, and managers who carry on the businesses would all remain also, and could just as well and as profitably be employed by society as they now are by the private capitalist. This point has been so well expressed in a recent magazine article by Mr. G. Balfour Browne, a King's Counsel of high standing, that I make no apology for quoting his words:

"Socialism, as we have seen," he says, "is no longer a war against capital, for it recognises that no work can be done without an expensive equipment. Before we can put the poor to work we must have raw material, we must have the machinery which with the help of labour is to produce the finished article: but it is a war against the holding of capital in private hands, and the payment of profits to those who hold the capital, instead of to the State which ought to hold the capital. Take a simple illustration. If a Gas Company exists in a town, it supplies gas to those who require that kind of illuminant, and the persons who use the gas are benefited thereby, for the company can produce and sell gas much more cheaply than the individuals could supply themselves. But the company spends its money not to benefit the consumer, but to secure what is called a return on its capital … This profit comes out of the pockets of the consumers of gas, and is regarded by the Socialists in the light of a tax. One thing is certain, and that is, that if the capital for the enterprise had been raised by the municipal corporation of the town, and the undertaking had been carried on as efficiently in the hands of the corporation as in the hands of the company, the profits resulting from the manufacture and distribution of gas might have gone into the public purse and been applied by the town to the reduction of rates, or they might have been given to the consumers of gas by reduction of the price of gas. In either of these events the public would have been the gainers, and the only losers would have been the shareholders in the company, who would not have found a profitable investment for their money.

"Now a precisely similar course of reasoning is applicable to any private ownership. Presumably a man holds land in order that he may receive the profits. A manufactory is erected with a view to gain; a railway is made by shareholders in order that they may reap a harvest of profit. Ships are sailed, banks established with the same object in view. If all these enterprises are profitable in the hands of private enterprise, it is obvious that the gains of such undertakings find their way into private pockets, and come out of the pockets of the public who use the land, who buy the manufactured article, who travel on the railway, who pay the freight, or who borrow from the bank. The desire of the Labourist is that all these profits should find their way into the public purse, and be disbursed for the benefit of the public. The foundation of this claim to appropriate all these means of production, distribution, and exchange is that the profits have not been created by the capitalist, but by the workmen, and consequently they belong to Labour and not to wealth.

"But the argument goes further. It is pointed out that the tax which is levied every year by the land-owner in the form of rent for farms, or ground-rent for 'stands' in cities, the interest on the public debt, the profits upon such enterprises as those we have referred to, as they have to be paid by the people, have to be in the first instance earned by the people, and that this system is equivalent to the *corvée,* for the workman has to work about one-third of his whole time for himself and his family, and about two-thirds of his whole time to pay these taxes to the rich. It is true that the workman would even in the case of a Collectivist State have to toil a portion of his time to pay rent, but the rent would go to the State, and therefore belong to him. He might have to work to pay interest on the public debt, but it would be a debt that had been incurred by him, and not, as our existing debt is, a debt incurred by capitalists in the interests of capital. He might have to labour to replace machinery, and even to pay a sinking fund; but the machinery would be his own, and he and his class would be the beneficiaries when the sinking fund had paid off the capital cost of the establishment. In this way, it is argued that under the present system the wage-earner is not his own property. For two-thirds of his time he is a slave, labouring not for himself but for others, and

Socialism is to emancipate him and let men in future own their own bodies and souls."[1]

This, coming as it does from an avowed opponent of Socialism, shows the common sense side of the movement. If the Community, through its elected representative institutions, national and municipal, can dispense with the private capitalist and landowner in the matter of houses, gas, water, electricity, tramways, insurance, why not also in such other essentials of life as bread, clothing, and furniture? If the State can build battleships and make swords, why not also trading ships and ploughshares? Since the State conveys letters and parcels and telegrams, why not also coal and wool and grain? And if the State insists upon owning telegraph lines, why not also railway lines? And if the railways, why not the coal mines from whence the power is drawn which sets the engines in motion? And if the coal mines, why not the ironworks and engineering shops in which the raw materials for the rails and the engines and the trucks are produced and fashioned into shape? When the State enters upon business in any department there is no logical halting-place short of complete State Socialism, and the further extension of its trading activities is purely a question of utility. Attempts to draw imaginary lines of demarcation between what is properly State and what private spheres of business influence, always break down hopelessly

[1] Article in *National Review* for November 1906.

when put to the test of principle. If water be a necessity of life, a common requirement of all, and therefore its supply a proper undertaking for the municipality, then so also is bread. Time was when water was not supplied through a monopoly granted either to a company or a municipality, as is now almost universally the case, and in those days each individual had to arrange for a supply as best he could. Experience showed, however, that the public convenience and the public health would both be gainers by making the supply of water a public concern, and no one nowadays challenges the wisdom of this step. Municipal milk depots are now, and for similar reasons, becoming common, and the beneficial results, on the health of infants especially, are such as to make the extension of this form of municipal trading a certainty.

In this connection it is interesting to recall the fact that municipalities in thus extending the sphere of their activities are but reverting to a sound rule of self-government of an earlier period. One reason for the extraordinary growth of cities in the Middle Ages was not merely that life was more secure within than without their walls, but also that the interests and welfare of the citizens were more carefully safeguarded. In very ancient times, in the palmy days that is to say of Greece and Rome, something closely akin to Communism seems to have obtained. In Sparta there were not only common lands, but also a common table, whilst dogs and horses were practically common property also. The common tables were kept supplied by each citizen contributing an equal quota.

Attendance at them was compulsory, and it was an offence for any one to "fatten like voracious animals in private." Sparta, which kept its Communism almost to the end, was also the Republic from which came the immortal heroes who made the pass of Thermopylae one of the great inspirations of the world. When, however, Communism was abandoned, and individuals began to amass fortunes, decay set in and Greece became a tributary to Rome. So long as the lands of Rome remained common property, power and prosperity belonged to the people. Wealth derived from conquered territories led to the growth of a wealthy class who made inroads upon old customs, and finally converted the public lands into large private estates and reduced the peasantry to bondage and beggary, and Rome fell. True, it may be alleged that in both these instances the benefits of communal property were confined to the comparatively few free citizens, and that the great army of working slaves, who had no rights, did not share in its benefits. This, however, in no way affects my argument, which is that with the growth of Capitalistic Individualism, and the accumulation of large fortunes, dry rot sets in, patriotism departs, and ruin overtakes the erstwhile most powerful peoples.

Coming nearer to our own times, we have still more evidence of a fairly well-developed communal life producing marvellous results. The great cities of the Middle Ages, now the show places of the world, were all built at a time when every private interest was held in subordination to the common weal. There were, primarily the Guilds, the trade unions of the period, in which the craftsmen were banded together for mutual aid and support. These undertook and carried through great public works, churches, town halls, bridges, and the like under the direct authorisation of the Town Council. There were town lands on which the town shepherds attended to the flocks and herds of their fellow-citizens. The markets, bridges, houses, and public buildings were nearly all communal property. So were the harbours and quays, and, sometimes at least, the vessels lying in them. But the town went much further than this in its care for the citizens. One of the fundamental principles of city government, as stated by one investigator, was to provide for "the common first food and lodging of poor and rich alike." It was a crime, punishable sometimes by death, to "forestall" the market. That is to say, any one going outside the city walls, or even beyond the boundaries of the market place, to purchase food, fuel, or raiment on terms and conditions not open to every citizen, was guilty of committing a felonious act. The citizen purchasing for his own use had the first claim upon the market, and after him the retail tradesman. It was another offence to buy goods wholesale in order to sell to retail traders. Middlemen were accounted no better than the common cutpurse, and treated accordingly. Any one discovered trying to create a corner in food was deemed a greater scourge than the highway robber, and incurred the death penalty for his pains. When food was scarce it had to be shared, each receiving according to his needs, whilst even in times of plenty prices were fixed by town officials, the "Mayor and two discreet men," so as to ensure that no more than an honest profit would be exacted. But even this does not exhaust the activities of the medieval town. There is documentary evidence extant to show that during the sixteenth century the town itself did the buying and distributing of food and fuel, probably, though not always, through the Trade Guilds. From London to Thurso, and from Neath to Waterford, this practice seems to have been common. The town saw that the goods made and sold were honest in workmanship and material, and that the prices charged the consumer were fair. Finally, the town provided rational amusement for the people in the form of concerts, plays, games, and the like. The men of these periods do not appear to have suffered either in character or public spirit from all this Socialist coddling. The cathedrals of our own and other lands, or such of them as remain, testify to the spirit of beauty which animated them as well as to the enduring quality of their craftsmanship. The ruined castles are monuments to their public spirit, since it was they who overthrew the war barons of that age and helped to give freedom to the land serfs. They kept kings at bay and refused to pay taxes in the levying of which they had had no say, and thus led to Parliament being formed. They were the real custodians and champions of freedom, largely because their civic institutions protected the liberty of each individual.

The modern Municipal Socialist is thus seen to be no rash innovator, venturing into an unknown sphere of public work, but only reverting back to a type of which he need not be ashamed. When he seeks to bring the necessaries as well as the conveniences of life under public ownership and control, he is but seeking to resuscitate a phase of British life which produced great and good results in the past. When the produce of the Village Commune was sold direct to the consumer in the municipal market of the neighbouring town, there was such prosperity and fulness of life in our country as it has not known since, and it was only when this condition of things and all that it stood for was destroyed by the intrigues of kings and their allies that poverty and poor laws came into being. The modern Socialist has the further assurance that the causes which led to the overthrow of such Communism as there was in town and country are not likely to operate again. Commercialism, with the form of Individualism which it carried with it, has now run its course and exhausted itself. It is now the receding, not the advancing power. The trend of the age is away from the arid realm in which Mammonism has so long held sway, and the tide of opinion is advancing strongly in the direction of a more human epoch. Wearied with its vain efforts to find happiness in money-making, mankind is now returning to its older and wiser self and is seeking to find in service that content and peace of mind which selfishness has failed to give.

CHAPTER 3

SOCIALISM AND
THE STATE

THE STATE, AS already stated, is what its people make it. Its institutions are necessarily shaped to further and protect the interests of the dominant influence. Whilst a landed nobility reigned supreme, the interests of that class were the one concern of the State. Subsequently with the growth of a commercial and trading class, which, when it became strong enough, insisted upon sharing the power of the State with the landed aristocracy, many of the old laws passed by the landlords in restraint of trade were modified. Now that the working-class is the dominant power, potentially at least, it logically and inevitably follows that that class will also endeavour to so influence the State as to make it protect their interests. As the political education of the working-class progresses, and they begin to realise what are the true functions of the State, their power will be exerted in an increasing degree in the direction of transforming the State from a property-preserving to a life-preserving institution. The fundamental fact which the working-class is beginning to recognise is that property, or at least its possession, is power. This is an axiom which admits of no contradiction. So long as property, using the term to mean land and capital, is in the hands of a small class, the rest of the people are necessarily dependent upon that class. A Democracy, therefore, has no option but to seek to transform these forms of property, together with the power inherent in them, from private to public possession. Opinion may differ as to the methods to be pursued in bringing about the change, but concerning its necessity there are no two opinions in the working-class movement. When land and capital are the common property of all the people class distinctions, as we know them at present, will no longer exist. The Mind will then be the standard by which a man's place among his fellows will be determined.

Socialist tactics have been as fruitful a cause of controversy as Socialism itself. In the early stages of the movement, at a time when the franchise was limited to the propertied classes and the working-class exercised practically no influence in the councils of the nation, the Socialist saw no means by which his purpose could be achieved save by revolution. The early, and in many respects the greatest, writers on Socialism frankly proclaimed armed revolution as being an essential part of their Socialist theories. They pictured the wealthy growing wealthier and the poor poorer, until a moment when, their poverty and suffering unendurable, the working-class would rise in wild revolt and overthrow the system which oppressed them. The advocates of this school, of whom some few still remain, did not admit the possibility of Socialism being gradually incorporated into the life of the nation. For a number of years the late William Morris, the greatest man whom the Socialist movement has yet claimed in this country, held and openly preached this doctrine of cataclysmic upheaval and sudden over-throw of the ruling classes, although in the closing years of his life he frankly threw it over. By this school of thinkers reforms for the amelioration of the lot of the people were anathematised as the wiles of the enemy to withdraw their attention from Socialism and make them contented with their lot as wage slaves. Let the Social sore bleed, they said, in effect, that all its ghastly horror may be brought home to the conscience of the nation; and the more miserable the lot of the workers the sooner would the revolution come. These tactics, however, have now been openly abandoned by the Socialist leaders in every constitutionally governed country. In Germany more social reforms for the benefit of the working-class have been enacted by the State than in any country in Europe, and it is in Germany where Socialism has made, and continues to make, greatest progress. France makes a good second in both respects. It is the intelligent fairly well-off artisan in Great Britain who responds most readily to the Socialist appeal, and it is the slum vote which the Socialist candidate fears most. In order to be effectually discontented, said Thorold Rogers, a people must be prosperous: when misery revolts it strikes blindly, and is generally restrained.

The modern Socialist recognises that a people depressed, weakened, and enervated by poverty and toil are more likely to sink into a nation of spiritless serfs than to rise in revolt against their lot. Experience also has shown that just in proportion as the lot of the worker is improved and his intelligence quickened, so does he become discontented and anxious for still further improvement. This is in accordance with all we know of the law of progress, and finds illustration on every hand. Further, it is now recognised that the progress of an idea in time influences even those whose interests are threatened by its success. No better illustration of this could be found than that supplied by the progress of the agitation against landlordism in Ireland. For generations the landlords of that country waged a relentless and unceasing war against its people. So bad did the condition of the peasantry become, that at length the State intervened to prevent their being altogether exterminated. Fair rents, fixity of tenure, and compensation for improvement gave the peasants of Ireland a new hope, and as that hope grew so did their strength increase and their agitation develop until there came a time at the beginning of the present century when the landlord class frankly admitted that dual control was no longer possible, and their one concern came to be, what were the best terms for themselves upon which it could be brought to an end? In like manner it is conceivable that the transference of industries from private hands to the State will be a gradual and peaceful process. Already, in fact, the process has advanced to a considerable stage. The property held and worked and controlled by municipalities already exceeds £500,000,000 sterling in value, and is being added to yearly. This process has but to continue long enough to ensure that every industry will pass under public control, and thus State Socialism will become an accomplished fact, by a gradual process of easy transition.

A recognition of this fact has brought about a complete change in Socialist tactics. With the enfranchisement of the masses it is recognised that the ballot is much more effective than the barricade. The mere weight of numbers on the side of a reform produces a psychological influence which acts upon the minds of rulers, and so soon as Socialism becomes popular, or even before then, when it is recognised by thinkers that Socialism offers the one chance left of saving our civilisation from being destroyed by wealth and poverty, great statesmen and philosophers will arise and take their stand boldly with the people in their fight for industrial freedom. Wycliffe, John Ball, Gerrard Winstanley, Sir Thomas More, Robert Owen, Ernest Jones, Charles Kingsley, Frederic Denison Maurice, Frederic Harrison, Cardinal Manning, and William Morris, are among the names which occur to me as being of the type I have in my mind. The workers of Greece had their Solon, of Sparta their Lycurgus, of Italy their Spartacus, of Germany their Huss in the hour of their social need, and the mould from which these Social Giants was formed cannot have been altogether destroyed.

In Great Britain two sets of influences are at work bringing the more intellectually minded of the middle-class over to Socialism. There is the increasing tension required in the conduct of business which so saps a man's energies as to leave him little of either time or inclination for the cultivation of any other than the business faculty. A tendency to revolt against this is a well-marked feature of the social life of our time. Of what use is it, ask these slaves of the ledger, to spend the greater part of a lifetime in acquiring a competency only to find after it has been acquired that its acquisition has taken all the savour of enjoyment out of life? It is surprising the charm which Socialism has for men and women of this type. Others come to Socialism through intellectual conviction and humanitarian promptings. The terrible lot of the people, from which there is no way of escape, harries their feelings and overrides all consideration of their own selfish material interests. Kinship with their fellows is more to them than their rent-rolls or their scrip, and these too, in gradually increasing numbers, are boldly championing the Socialist cause. When the Socialist propaganda takes more cognisance of this class and makes special efforts to reach them, especially in their school or college days, a rich harvest of results will be reaped.

But it is to the working-class itself that we must look for changing the system of production and making it a means of providing for the healthy human need of all the people. This is so not only because of their numbers but also because unless they consciously set themselves to win Socialism it can never be won. It is, in the fullest sense of a very much abused phrase, a People's Cause. When it has been won it will be their fight which has won it; should it never be won, and should our Western civilisation totter on until it falls into the depths of a merciful oblivion, that too will be their doing, and be due entirely to their not having had the courage and the intelligence to put up a fight strong enough to save it and themselves.

Hitherto the workers have been content to ask for small reforms; now they are realising that private property is the enemy they have to encounter. The property question is the issue which is creating a new political cleavage in the State. Somewhat dimly at present, but with growing clearness of vision, the worker begins to see that he will remain a menial, outcast and forlorn, until he has made himself master of the machine he tends and the soil he tills. Hence the growth of Socialism.

What indications, then, are there that the working-class are likely to prove equal to the occasion, and play the heroic part which is theirs in the evolution of a juster state of society? I deem the signs many and great.

Once again the instinct of the worker has proved itself a surer guide than the philosophies of the Schoolmen. At a time when Individualism, imported from France by the way, was taking firm hold over the minds of Radical economists and philosophers in Great Britain, the workmen were flying directly in the teeth of all that was being preached to them. Individualism meant, *inter alia,* the absolute freedom of a man to sell his labour in the way which his own individual interests might decide him to deem the best, and anything which in any way interfered with this freedom of action on his part was, he was assured by the wise men, a thing accursed. Further, he was assured, that any interference with the free play of capital would bring heavy punishment in its train. All the time that this was being proclaimed to the workman, he, in the face of public opinion and of legal enactment, was sturdily building up his trade-union organisation, the primary object of which was to restrain individual action, and put a curb upon capital when it sought to impose too harsh conditions upon his labour. For nearly three quarters of a century the unequal struggle for the legal recognition of Trade Unions and the right to combine was kept up between the voteless workman on the one side and the forces of law, savagely administered, and public opinion on the other. The workman won, although not until he had been enfranchised in the big towns.

There are now two and a quarter million trade-union workers organised for mutual aid and support, and a feeling of solidarity is growing inside the movement which is full of promise. Just as the small business is being swallowed up in the big Combine, so are the separate Unions drawing together into Federations, and these in turn are uniting into one all-embracing Federation. The great Co-operative movement and the Friendly Orders for succour in sickness and old age, are further evidences of the instinct of the working-class for combined action. It may be alleged, and with some truth, that no great Altruistic ideal underlies any of these movements, and that at most they are merely forms of insurance against eventualities. That, however, is beside the point. The fact which I am seeking to illustrate is that the working-class is developing a sense of solidarity, of standing by each other, and of sinking self in what is meant to be the good of all. A people which has got thus far will be prepared to go a good deal further as its outlook broadens, its understanding deepens, and as the occasion demands. The greatest sign of hope of all, however, is the evolution of a political Labour Party. Here also the intuition of the worker is carrying him away from the tutelage of his would-be mentors. In at least thirty constituencies at the General Election of 1906 his vote returned Labour men to Parliament, many of them avowed Socialists, and all of them independent. In almost as many more constituencies similar candidates only just failed of being successful. The evidence which this fact affords of the growing faith of the worker in himself and of his determination to hew a pathway through the briar entanglement in which he finds himself is self-evident. Thus on every side we are made aware of the growing consciousness of the working-class movement and of the earnestness by which it is characterised. Already it is largely a Socialist movement, and is in continual process of becoming more so. With the speculative side of Socialism the average man with us has but small concern; it is its common sense which appeals to him. By inherited instinct we are all Communists at heart; and if the isolated Ego of self gets the upper hand for a time he produces results so terrifying that the mistake of allowing him to rule is speedily made apparent, and we begin to seek a way whereby we may return to the kindly sway of the spirit of Altruism. For a full rounded century the gospel of Selfishness has held sway, and under it the nation has stumbled on from one depth to another until it has reached the verge of a precipice from the void of which there can be no re-ascent should we be dragged over. Poverty, physical deterioration, insanity, are evils which no nation can suffer and yet live. They are all three the direct product of the competitive system of wealth production; and it is, or should be, the first and most urgent business of the State to uproot the upas tree which bears such deadly fruit.

CHAPTER 4

SOCIALISM AND CHRISTIANITY

S OCIALISM, LIKE EVERY other problem of life, is at bottom a question of ethics or morals. It has mainly to do with the relationships which should exist between a man and his fellows. Civilisation, even in its lowest forms, necessitates that people should live together as an organism since only thus is life with any degree of security and of intellectual companionship possible. As Kropotkin has shown, the weakest and most inoffensive of the lower animals are able to hold their own against the strongest and most ferocious by congregating together in societies. Since, then, community of life in one form or another is inevitable, Socialism challenges that conception of Society which regards each unit as being at war with every other and which raises artificial barriers between individuals and classes, and thus hinders that free intercourse and community of feeling and interest which is so necessary to the promotion of happiness. If under the present system the poor are made prisoners by their poverty, the rich are made no less so by their wealth. Every relationship in life is vitiated by the false basis upon which Society rests.

The charge that Socialism is a materialistic creed comes with a bad grace from those whose every waking hour is spent either in striving to accumulate wealth at the expense of their neighbours, or in sensuous and luxurious enjoyment of the pleasures of life. It cannot be too emphatically stated that Socialism takes no more cognisance of the religious opinions of its adherents than does either Liberalism or Conservatism. It would, however, be an easy task to show that Communism, the final goal of Socialism, is a form of Social Economy very closely akin to the principles set forth in the Sermon on the Mount. Christ recognised clearly that the possession of private property came between a man and his welfare both for time and eternity; and every great religious and moral teacher whom the world has ever known has denounced wealth and eulogised poverty. They have done so, not in the sense that poverty, meaning the absence of the necessaries and conveniences of life, is a thing either good or desirable in itself, but to emphasise the fact that riches and property are things inherently evil when personally owned and possessed. We have but to listen to a sermon in any church in Christendom to learn how far this interpretation of Christianity is opposed to modern religious opinion, and yet I hold it to be the doctrine upon which Christianity and Socialism are alike based. The Mosaic laws for the regulation of the holding of land and the treatment of the poor and the unfortunate cannot perhaps be described as Socialistic in the modern sense of the word. When we remember, however, that they were framed to meet the needs of a people just emerging from the nomadic pastoral state, in which Communism of a crude but effective sort had been practised, and were intended to put a check upon the growing rapacity of those early Individualists who were adding field to field and plying the usurer's calling, we see that they were quite as drastic in their way as are many of the Socialist proposals of our day. Usury was prohibited, land could neither be sold outright nor held for more than a limited period as security for debt; even the debtor was freed from all obligations when the year of jubilee came round. The prophets and preachers of the pre-Christian era were loud in their denunciations of the folly of those who expected happiness from riches. They beheld the tears of the oppressed, and saw that on the side of the oppressors there was wealth and power. They declared that the profit of the earth was for all, and that even the king was dependent upon the field for his daily food. Men were heaping up riches which they could not enjoy and were only thereby adding to their own hurt, labouring for the wind. Social equality and fierce denunciations of the rich form the staple of the writings we are now taught to look upon as having been inspired. As Renan has it: The prophets of Israel are fiery publicists of the description we should now call

Socialists or Anarchists. They are fanatical in their demands for social justice, and proclaim aloud that, if the world is not just nor capable of becoming just, it were better it were destroyed. The rich man was an impious extortioner, whilst he who deprived the workman of his wages was stigmatised as a murderer. Clearly the modern system of wealth accumulation, which is rooted and grounded in land monopoly, usury, and the fleecing of the poor, finds no support in such teachings as are contained in the Old Testament Scriptures.

The Sermon on the Mount, whilst it perhaps lends but small countenance to State Socialism, is full of the spirit of pure Communism. Nay, in its lofty contempt for thrift and forethought, it goes far in advance of anything ever put forward by any Communist, ancient or modern. Christ's denunciations of wealth are only equalled by the fierceness of the diatribes which He levelled against the Pharisees. It was St. Paul who enunciated the doctrine that he who would not work neither should he eat, whilst St. James in his Epistle rivals the old prophets in his treatment of those who grow rich at the expense of the poor. Contrary to the generally accepted opinion, it is now known that Communism in goods was practised by Christians for at least three hundred years after the death of Christ. Almost without exception, the early Christian Fathers whose teachings have come down to us spoke out fearlessly against usury, which includes interest also, and on the side of Communism. They proclaimed that, inasmuch as nature had provided all things in common, it was sinful robbery for one man to own more than another, especially if that other was in want. The man who gathered much whilst others had not enough, was a murderer. The poor had a right to their share of everything there was, which is different from the charity so common nowadays. If a man inherited wealth he was, if not a robber himself, but the recipient of stolen goods, since no accumulation of wealth could be come by honestly. To those who said that the idleness of the poor was the cause of their poverty, St. John Chrysostom replied that the rich too were idlers living on their plunder.

For seven hundred years, says one authority, almost all the Fathers of the Church considered Communism the most perfect and most Christian form of Social organisation, and it was only after Christianity, from being the despised and persecuted creed of the poor, had become the official religion of the State, that opinion on this point began to undergo a change. Even then it was not until the thirteenth century that the Church came out into the open as a defender of property. All the great semi-religious semi-political movements from the twelfth to the seventeenth century, had a Communistic basis. In fact, there is good reason to believe that they had their origin in the teachings of the Weaving Friars, a semi-religious and strongly Communistic Trade Guild formed in Bruges by the

Flemish woollen weavers towards the end of the twelfth century. Whether this was so or not, this at least is not open to dispute, that the Peasant Revolt in England – led by John Ball, "the Mad Priest of Kent" – drew its inspiration from the Communistic teachings of Wycliffe; that when, ten years later, Bohemia was in revolt, the leader was John Huss the Communist; when in 1525 (April 2nd) the Peasants' War broke out simultaneously all over Germany, Saxony, and Switzerland, it was the teachings of Thomas Munster, the German Communist, which were, and rightly, credited with being the cause. The world-famous Anabaptist movement which followed was avowedly Communistic. All of these risings met with a common fate; Church and State combined their forces and suppressed them with even more than the usual savage barbarity and inhuman cruelty of the age.

During the Commonwealth period in England some 5000 of Cromwell's Roundheads tried to induce the Protector to adopt a Socialist constitution for the Commonwealth. We have Cromwell's own authority for saying that Lilburne's Levellers, as they were contemptuously nicknamed, wanted "to make the tenant as liberal a fortune as the landlord." Such rank heresy to the Commonwealth had of course to be stamped out at all costs, and Cromwell put as much energy into the work of putting down the Communists of his own ranks – though they had fought with him and for him – as he did into that for the suppression of

the rebellious Irish kernes. In fact, some of the shoot-
ings which took place read almost like scenes from the
horrors which accompanied the suppression of the
Commune of Paris in 1871. All this, it may truly be
said, is no evidence that Communism is the best form
of Government, but it is evidence so strong as to be
irrefutable that Christianity in its pristine purity had
Communism as its invariable outcome, and that for
nearly seventeen centuries the common people and
their leaders believed Communism and Christianity to
be synonymous terms. Incidentally it shows how little
modern churchgoers know of the history of their own
religion when they charge Socialism with being
anti-Christian.

Socialists, in common with the early Christian
fathers, recognise, that it is futile to proclaim fraternity
and community of interest unless they at the same time
provide the environment and conditions of life which
make these possible. It is a mockery to proclaim a high
ideal to people whilst supporting a system which makes
it impossible for the ideal ever to be realised. Let me
illustrate this by a simple illustration. It is estimated
that there are 120,000 women in the metropolis alone
living on the earnings of shame. Suppose some great
preacher, some modern Savonarola, to enter upon a
crusade amongst these women, and to succeed in
awakening within them – no difficult task by the way
– a desire to leave the life they now lead and to enter
upon one of honest work, where in all the land are

120,000 situations to be found to which they may turn? If those good folks who preach the higher life, leaving all worldly considerations out of account, will but master this simple elementary fact, many of the problems which now to them appear insoluble will have been solved. Men do not gather grapes from thorns, nor figs from thistles, and it is for this reason that Socialists concentrate their efforts upon a change of the system under which wealth is produced – and which enables the strong and the unscrupulous to prey upon the community and condemns the mass of the people to a life of toil and poverty – as an indispensable preliminary to that further development of the higher forms of life which they, in common with all reformers, desire to see. To the taunt that this is beginning at the wrong end, the obvious retort is that the other method has been tried for centuries with what results we know only too well. It is not without significance that many of the best known present-day leaders of religious thought are avowed Socialists in the modern sense of the word, and if they claim the right to call themselves Christian Socialists, no one who knows anything of the history of Christianity will challenge their right to use the prefix. My purpose in writing this chapter will have been served if I have succeeded in showing that the Socialist who denounces rent and interest as robbery, and who seeks the abolition of the system which legalises such, is in the true line of apostolic succession with the pre-Christian era prophets, with the Divine Founder of Christianity, and with those who for the first seven hundred years of the Christian faith maintained even to the death the unsullied right of their religious faith to be regarded as the Gospel of the poor. Surely if Socialism can enable man

To stand from fear set free, to breathe and wait,
To hold a hand uplifted over Hate,

it will be, if not a religion in itself, at least a hand-maiden to religion, and as such entitled to the support of all who pray for the coming of Christ's Kingdom upon earth. For—

Methinks, if nought be done to ease the pain,
The weariness, the hunger, and the fret
Of life on earth, there is no hope in heaven
For the dumb workers with dull crowded brain
And tired bodies that crave nought but sleep.

CHAPTER V

SOCIALISM AND THE WORKER

A CCORDING TO Professor Thorold Rogers the golden age of the English workman was the fifteenth century. Food was cheap, wages high, and an eight-hour day the rule. An artisan who boarded out had to pay from ninepence to one shilling per week for food and lodging, whilst his wages ranged from three shillings to four shillings per week of forty-eight hours. In 1495, according to the same authority, an artisan could provision his family for a whole year out of the earnings of ten weeks' work, whilst an agricultural labourer could do the same with fifteen weeks' work. It appears to have been common in those far-off days to pay for Sundays and holidays when there was no work done. Nor was this state of things peculiar to England. It is now known that a similar state of things obtained in France and Saxony. In the latter place we are told a stone mason in the fifteenth century could buy with his week's wages three sheep and one pair of shoes. There were in addition to Sundays thirty-four holidays or Church festivals in the course of the year

– eighty-six days in all on which no work was done, and in addition work ceased at four o'clock on Saturdays and on twenty-five other Fair days. Rogers particularly mentions the fifteenth and the first quarter of the sixteenth century as limiting the duration of this golden age. More recent investigations, however, have confirmed his guess that, taking Europe as a whole, it lasted from the beginning of the thirteenth to the middle of the fifteenth century, or roughly from two hundred to three hundred years, and there were neither Millionaires nor Paupers in those days, but a rude abundance for all. Two main causes seem to have been at work in producing it: the rising of the peasants in the country districts, and the growth of towns, with the free communal life which characterised them and the enormous areas of the Common lands. In addition, the Plague or Black Death and the wars of the period had thinned the population, and in the towns each trade was strongly protected by its Guild. Whatever these may have developed into in their later stages, they were originally the equivalent of our modern Trade Unions. It is interesting to note that we have records of these Unions as far back as history carries. Greece in its palmiest days knew their strength, as did also Rome when in the heyday of its power. The resurrected inscriptions on the walls of buried Pompeii include a nomination by the members of the Fishermen's Union of one of their number to a seat on the Board of Works, and of "Mrs. Cappella" to act as a magistrate.

Direct Labour Representation and Women Suffrage are thus shown to have quite a respectable antiquity to recommend them.

In England it took the State two hundred years to reduce the worker, town and country alike, from independent affluence to a poverty-stricken condition. Legislation for regulating wages and for chaining the worker to one parish, to fix the kind of cloth he should dress in, the number of hours he should work, and other like regulations intended to weaken the power of the working-class, had all been tried; but it was only when the land was taken from the peasants, the commons confiscated, and the Guilds broken up, and, finally, when the price of food had been doubled and quadrupled through the operations of a debased coinage, that success attended these maleficent acts. The Protestant Reformation, by despoiling the monasteries of their lands, the one refuge to which the needy worker could fly for succour, also told heavily against the poor, whilst the new gospel of individual salvation lent the sanction of religion to the selfish creed of each for himself which was then just beginning to assert itself as the dominant principle in business. Under its baneful influence old customs and habits and the old communal traditional life of the people in town and country were ruthlessly broken and destroyed, and that era of desolation and barren inhumanity entered upon from which we are now only just beginning to emerge. For, as I show in another chapter, the prosperity of the worker was coincident with, and its continuance in no small measure attributable to, a period chiefly remarkable for the strong element of Communism which characterised town and village life. If the Anabaptists and the various other sects who had sought to make Communism and Christianity synonymous terms had been washed out in a tempest of blood and flame, much of their spirit remained. It was not for nothing that John Ball and Wat Tyler had taught the peasantry of England the doctrine of the dignity of manhood and the emptiness of titles.

John Stuart Mill expressed a doubt whether all the mechanical inventions of the nineteenth century had lightened the labour of one human being. The social investigator of the twentieth century is prepared to affirm positively that the lot of the poor in normal times under Capitalism is worse than it ever could have been in normal times in any previous period in British history. Production, say the Fawcetts in their lectures on Social and Political subjects, has been stimulated beyond the expectations of the most sanguine; still, however, so far as the labourer is concerned, the age of golden plenty seems as remote as ever, and in the humble homes of the poor a no less constant war has to be waged against penury and want. This, however, is but half the truth. The conditions attendant upon poverty in these latter days are more demoralising than ever before. In the less complex life of former days the poor were more akin to other classes, and better able to help themselves. In the great vortex of modern life they are almost completely shut off from human fellowship. The stress and strain are so great, the organisation of Society so anarchic, that once a man gets down into the depths his chances of rising again are exceedingly remote.

I know that it is a commonplace of the Jeremiahs of every age to hold that the men of former ages were better than those of their own. In certain respects I confess that I rank with those who believe that we have deteriorated, especially in the sphere of intellect, since the days of our great-grandparents. The stage, the press, and the pulpit could easily be cited as evidence in support of this. The plays of Shakespeare were performed, even in his own day, to crowded audiences without the scenic effects and curtailment which are now necessary to make them acceptable to the modern playgoer. Any one familiar with the popular literature of the Radical and Chartist movements of the opening and middle years of last century will see how far its modern successor falls below the standard of those days. The solid sermon and newspaper articles of even half-a-hundred years ago would not now be tolerated; not because of their dulness, but because of the mental effort needed to follow and understand them. A snippety press and a sensational pulpit are outstanding marks of modern times. Nor are the reasons far to seek. Previous to the introduction of machinery and the factory system every workman was an individual.

They were not herded together in masses, regimented, numbered, and specialised. The blacksmith, the weaver, the carpenter, the shoemaker, and the tailor either worked direct for their own customers or for masters only a very small degree removed from themselves. A master was in those days more of a master workman than an employer. Each journeyman could confidently look forward to the time when he too would be a master. The master's income rarely exceeded by more than 20 per cent. the wage of his workmen, with whom he freely mingled both in work and play. It was only when machinery and the factory system were introduced that great fortunes began to be accumulated and masters and workmen separated into distinct classes with an ever-widening breach between them. When working for themselves, as a very large proportion of the old-time craftsmen did, they started work in the morning when it pleased them, broke off during the day as it suited them, and left off in the evening according to the necessities of the moment or their own whim or convenience. Each such man was his own master; he owned the tools wherewith he worked, and the product was his own property when completed. A man had some pride in the labour of his hands, some incentive to do his best, since his good name was at stake in every job he turned out. Under those conditions the tendency was to develop individuality. The free exchange of opinion which resulted from men of this type meeting together for a social glass or pipe developed an intellectuality which we look for in vain in the modern factory hand. Nor is this all. The uncertainty and irresponsibility of the modern workman's lot in life must produce evil effects upon his character.

We are all more or less the products of our environment, and modern workshop conditions are not conducive to the production of either intellect or individuality. The workman is called into the workshop when capital can profitably employ him, and turned adrift again the moment capital finds it can no longer turn his services to profitable account. He is not consulted as to when he shall be employed or when cast adrift. His necessities and those of his dependants are no concern of any one save himself. He has no right to employment, no one is under obligation to find him work, nor is he free to work for himself since he has neither the use of land nor the command of the necessary capital. He must be more or less of a nomad, ready to go at a moment's notice to where a job is vacant. He may be starving, but may not grow food; naked, but may not weave cloth; homeless, but may not build a house. When in work he has little if any say in the regulations which govern the factory, and none in deciding what work is to be done or how it is to be done. His duty begins and ends in doing as he is bid. To talk to a neighbour workman at the bench is an offence punishable by a fine; so, too, in some cases is whistling while at work. At a given hour in the morning the factory bell warns him that it is time to be inside the gate ready for the machines to start; at a set hour the bell or hooter calls him out to dinner and again recalls him to his task one hour later. He does not own the machines he manipulates, nor does he own the product of his labour. He is a hireling, and glad to be any man's hireling who will find him work. During one period when trade is good he is not only fully employed but has to work overtime; at another when trade is slack he is only partially employed, if employed at all. The result of all this is to produce demoralisation of the most fatal kind. There is no sense of unity between the man and his work. He can have no pride in it since there is nothing personal to him which will attach to it after it is finished. It will be sold he knows not by whom nor to whom. All day long he works under the eye of a taskmaster set over him to see that he does not shirk his duties. At the end of the week he is paid so many shillings for what he has done, and, naturally enough, his one concern is with the number of shillings he will receive. This is the cash nexus which binds him to his employer, who, by the way, is very likely a huge impersonal soulless concern known as a company. Of the individuals composing it he knows nothing, nor they of him.

There is no sense of honour or of Chivalry in business. A big wealthy concern will cheat its workpeople of their wages, or spend thousands in resisting the claim to compensation of some poor widow or orphan whose husband or father has been killed in their service. It is not that employers are inhuman; but their connection with their workpeople is a business one, from which every trace of human feeling has been carefully excluded.

Time has no birthday gifts for such as these,
A human herd of starved and stunted growth,
That knows not how to walk, to whom the speech
Of England, of the land that gave them birth,
Comes twisted, harsh and scarce articulate,
Whose minds lie fallow, while they chew the cud
Of hunger, darkness, impotence, disease.

As old age approaches – and for the workman this may mean anything over forty – a cold grey terror begins to take possession of his heart. Fight against it as he may, he cannot get away from the fact that within the circle of his acquaintance there are men just turned forty, as good workmen as himself, for whom the ordinary labour market no longer has any use. He knows his turn will also come some day. A slackness of trade, some petty offence which in a younger man would pass unnoticed, and out he goes to return no more. Then begins life's tragedy in grim earnest. From place to place he goes in search of a job. He knows himself to be still capable of much good work. To the business man forty-five is the period of life at which he is at his best; it is also the age at which a rising statesman enters upon his career, when the powers of the artist and the man of letters are at their fullest. But all this only adds bitterness to the cup of humiliation which the aged workman has now to drain to the dregs. Most large establishments have a standing order that no one over forty-five is to be given employment; with many the age limit is forty; whilst in one case to which publicity was recently given it is as low as thirty-five. And so the aged workman who has too much honour left to lie about his age and too much honesty to use hair dye, at last wearies of his vain quest for what will never again be his, a steady job at his own trade, and resorts to any odd job which turns up. As for savings to meet a case of this kind, that is usually quite out of the question. The thrifty, steady workman who is a member of a trade union and a benefit society is entitled to certain old age benefits, but these do not accrue until he is fifty-five or sixty; and although it is common to stretch the rules of these organisations to meet the more deserving cases, obviously the funds would not stand the strain of meeting all of them. Besides, not more than one half of the working people are in a position to make any such provision for old age. The earnings of the working-class only average about 21s. 6d. a week. That figure, be it remembered, is got by taking the total income of all who are not paid more than £160 a year and dividing it by the number of wage-workers. But low as this figure must appear to the comfortable classes, it does not reveal the whole truth. Knowing the facts both from personal experience and a thorough familiarity with the circumstances, I assert fearlessly that one half of the adult workers of Great Britain earn less than one pound per week, year in and year out, when in work. This leaves no margin for saving, nor does it provide even that subsistence wage which the economists are so fond of telling us competition will not fail to provide for the worker. Perhaps this can best be brought out by a reference to a work the conclusions of which have never been seriously challenged. In his painstaking and exhaustive inquiry into the condition of the people of York, a typical industrial town, Mr. Seebohm Rowntree arrived at pretty much the same conclusion as was reached by Mr. Charles Booth when he made a similar inquiry concerning the life of the people of London. Mr. Rowntree says that in York the minimum upon which bare physical efficiency can be maintained is 21s. 8d. a week, and that in a year of abounding trade and prosperity he found that forty-five per cent. of the working-class, taking their income from every source and treating the family earning as a unit for the purpose of the calculation, were receiving less than this sum, and consequently were in poverty. Here is his definition of poverty:–

It is thus seen that *the wages paid for unskilled labour in York are insufficient to provide food, shelter, and clothing adequate to maintain a family of moderate size in a state of bare physical effi-*

ciency. It will be remembered that the above estimates of necessary minimum expenditure are based upon the assumption that the diet is even less generous than that allowed to able-bodied paupers in the York Workhouse, and that *no allowance is made for any expenditure other than that absolutely required for the maintenance of merely physical efficiency.*

And let us clearly understand what "merely physical efficiency" means. A family living upon the scale allowed for in this estimate must never spend a penny on railway fare or omnibus. They must never go into the country unless they walk. They must never purchase a halfpenny newspaper or spend a penny to buy a ticket for a popular concert. They must write no letters to absent children, for they cannot afford to pay the postage. They must never contribute anything to their church or chapel, or give any help to a neighbour which costs them money. They cannot save, nor can they join sick club or trade union, because they cannot pay the necessary subscriptions. The children must have no pocket money for dolls, marbles, or sweets. The father must smoke no tobacco, and must drink no beer. The mother must never buy any pretty clothes for herself or for her children, the character of the family wardrobe as for the family diet being governed by the regulation, Nothing must be bought but that which is absolutely necessary for the maintenance of physical health, and what is bought must be of the plainest and most economical description. Should a child fall ill, it must be attended by the parish doctor; should it die it must be buried by the parish. Finally the wage-earner must never be absent from his work for a single day.

If any of these conditions are broken, the extra expenditure is met, *and can only be met,* by limiting the diet, or, in other words, by sacrificing physical efficiency ... It cannot, therefore, be too clearly understood, nor too emphatically repeated, *that whenever a worker having three children dependent on him, and receiving not more than 21s. per week, indulges in any expenditure beyond that required for the barest physical needs, he can do so only at the cost of his own physical efficiency, or of that of some members of his family.*

The italics are the author's. These, then, are the causes which have led to the intellectual and moral deterioration of the working-class. Under all these circumstances the workmen would have been different from every other created being had he not deteriorated physically and mentally. True, we have got over the worst in this respect, and already a very decided change is noticeable among the younger men. From 1780 to 1850 was a transition period, and then the process of demoralisation was doing its worst. The generation following inherited all the bad effects of the conditions which had been prevailing, but the young generation of to-day, thoroughly in touch with their environment and intelligently conscious of the causes which make them the slaves of the machine, are in full revolt; and just as the awakened serfs of the thirteenth century carved their way to comparative freedom and prosperity, so too shall the awakening proletariat of the twentieth century. But the foundation on which they shall build their industrial freedom shall be more abiding than any which has gone before. When the modern industrial movement reaches fruition, land, capital, and the State itself shall all be owned and controlled by the useful classes. There shall be no longer an exploiting class left to reduce the workers again to penury and want by the methods which, as we have seen, were so successful in the Middle Ages. Socialism, by taking away the power to exploit, ensures permanent freedom for all.

CHAPTER 6

SOCIALISM AND THE WOMAN QUESTION

I N A STATE OF Society in which strength and brutality are the ruling factors, the gentle and weak
must go to the wall. At a very early stage, therefore, in the evolution of the race woman must have
come under the subjection of man. It is a great defect
to be weak, says Letourneau, even in our most civilised
societies, but in the early stage of human development
it is an unpardonable wrong. Woman's recurring
periods of maternity, and the love for her offspring
which grew out of it, must, apart from other reasons,
have handicapped her seriously, especially during the
nomadic period. Be the cause what it may, we know
that amongst savage races the woman is the drudge,
the beast of burden who does all the hard and disagreeable work, whilst her lord and master hunts and
fishes, or smokes and basks in the sun. She is, in these
cases, treated as a rule as being on the same level with
the slaves. She has no rights, and may be maltreated or
killed by her paramour without let or hindrance.
Curiously enough, women seem to have been the first

form of private property. She it was who first "belonged" to some man. After a time, when the family became more or less of an institution, it was through the mother that property descended, a form, by the way, which seems to have survived until quite a recent period amongst Celtic peoples. The mythical lore of most nations, especially the Celts, frequently shows the woman as the hero, which may however be simply, like so many other things in mythology, a reminiscence from some golden age of humanity which has completely vanished from our ken. Be that as it may, so far as history shows, woman has all down through the ages been the burden-bearer. Occasionally we get glimpses of what appears to be a new era dawning for women, as when Mrs. Cappella is being nominated for election to the Board of Education in Pompeii; but a little more investigation reveals the fact that these favoured women of antiquity were frequently the courtesans and not the douce mothers of families. The position of the courtesan in the ancient empires of the East has never been fully explained. It is certain, however, that she occupied a place of honour and was accorded rights, liberties, and privileges which were jealously withheld from her virtuous sister. May I suggest that her economic independence probably affords a key to the explanation? It is the absence of this which, whether in man or woman, leads to their captivity by others on whom they have to depend for a livelihood, and the married woman is nearly always, unfortunately, a dependent. Even in those instances where she is not, the force of habit produces in her the same attitude of mind and will as is shown by those who are.

The position of women would, I submit, be revolutionised by Socialism. The Sex problem is at bottom the Labour problem. All questions of women's rights and wrongs, including the marriage laws, resolve themselves in their final analysis into this – that she is economically dependent upon man. In the sphere of industry woman is beginning to take an ever-increasing part, and in many cases is being used as a weapon wherewith to beat down the wages of men. In one or two instances, especially in the textile industries, where the trade union organisation is strong, women receive equal rates of pay when doing the same work as men, but this is the exception. In the East End of London, and, in fact, in the east of every great city, there is a class of women workers whose condition is too pitiable for language to describe. They occupy the lowest place of any in the industrial scale, and seem, at present, the most helpless and consequently the most hopeless portion of the community. I was not, however, thinking of the sweated industrial woman only when I spoke of economic dependence. The daughter of the middle-class man, trained to play the fine lady, is usually dependent upon a successful marriage for the means of keeping up her position. In the ranks of the working-class the same thing applies. The average young woman of the working-class, who is not herself employed in some well-paid occupation, has nothing but marriage to which to look forward. She gives herself and all she has or is in exchange for such board as her husband's means permit. So long as the present system of wealth production and distribution continues, it is difficult to say how this could be changed. In ancient Rome, under Augustus, the law *Julia et Papia Poppoea* compelled a wealthy father to give his marriageable daughter a substantial dowry. Even were this revived, it could only benefit a privileged few. Recently, proposals have been seriously put forward for the endowment of Motherhood by the State. This, however, has been more in connection with a desire to prevent the race suicide which is threatened by the way in which the families of the well-to-do and more intelligent members of the community are being limited to two or three children, than from any real desire to improve the mother's position as a woman. The old-fashioned type of woman is becoming scarce. She was not only willing to bear a large family, but in addition to play a part in the domestic economy of the nation the value of which has not, I think, been sufficiently appreciated. The type of woman whom I have in my mind was she, who, in addition to being a wife and the mother of eight or ten children, also undertook the duties of housekeeper, cook, tablemaid, nurse, charwoman, washerwoman, laundrymaid, and general slavey in a house of one or two rooms, on a wage of from 20s. to 30s. a week – often on less. The best of these working wives and mothers are the most remarkable instances on record of patient uncomplaining industry and inherited skill. For not only did they get through their work, but they performed each and every one of their multifarious tasks as though it had been their one and only occupation. Oh the pathos of those bright, clean, bien, couthie cottage homes, with the thrifty mother never idle, and never fussed, patching, darning, knitting or sewing, keeping the cradle gently rocking with a light touch of her foot as she crooned some old ballad or soothing lullaby to keep her last born quiet, whilst she plied her needle and shears! She ruled her little kingdom in love and gentle firmness, often, I fear, without that appreciation which was her due. She was a National Asset of priceless worth. But these too are going out, as the handicraftsmen have gone, and their place soon shall know them no more, and the world is growing a colder and poorer place for lack of them. Capitalism has much to answer for.

The modern woman is of quite a different type. She prefers the comparative freedom of the factory or the shop or office, to the eternal drudgery and espionage of domestic service. When married she gets from the market many of the wares which her forebear made with her own hands. Knitting and sewing are not to her taste, and she considers herself disgraced if her family exceeds two or three children. She is infected by the restless spirit of the age, and is no longer the

contented domestic drudge so common a generation or
so ago. She is clamouring for the vote, and will ere long
succeed in winning it. Whether it will realise all she
expects from it when it has been won is more than
doubtful, but at least it will place her on terms of political equality with man.

Now I regard all this, with all its drawbacks, as a
healthy sign of the times – as an indication, in fact, of
better times in store for mankind. Unrest and discontent are the heralds of coming change, the forerunners
of reform. The more women agitate, the deeper they
probe into their grievances, the more clearly will it be
borne in upon them that the real root cause of all their
trouble is their economic dependence upon man. Under
Socialism when the woman, whether as wife, mother or
worker, will have a claim in her own right to a share in
the national wealth, she will at once emerge into greater
freedom. In choosing a mate she will no longer be
driven by hard economic necessity to accept the most
eligible offer from the worldly point of view, but will be
guided exclusively by all-compelling love and the need
for congenial companionship. Biologists tell us that it is
to natural selection we owe the development and
improvement of the species. The strong, good-looking
male attracts the best of the females, and thus the best
qualities on both sides get transmitted to offspring and
are by them passed on to succeeding generations until
they become permanently incorporated. This is the real
struggle there is in the animal kingdom, the struggle of

the best for partnership with the best. Dr. Karl Pearson, and other authorities, have been warning us that the unfit and the less fit are multiplying in Great Britain at a rate out of all proportion to the more fit, and that in this direction also we are making at headlong pace for race suicide. This too is purely a question of economics. The very poor have no sense of responsibility, and give a looser rein to the passions than their better fed, housed, clothed, conditioned and, consequently, better controlled neighbours. I think too it may be found to be a biological fact that a badly nutritioned, and consequently ill-conditioned loose organism is more prolific than one more firmly knit; and also that as intellect grows the reproductive organs become less fruitful. Be that as it may, one thing is certain: were women freed from their economic bondage to man, they would have a freer choice than at present in the selection of a father for their children, and the tendency would then be for the less fit to get left and the more fit taken, and, as a consequence, and without any outside interference, such as is sometimes suggested, the race would begin to improve straight away.

For woman, as for man therefore, it is to Socialism we must look. No reform of the marriage law, or of the franchise laws, will of themselves materially alter her condition. At best the vote is but a means to an end, and the end is freedom, and freedom means the right to live and to the means of life in exchange for the performance of some duty to the community. The time will come when motherhood will be regarded as the most sacred of all duties, and will be rewarded accordingly.

Socialism means, then, that the sexes shall meet on terms of freedom and equality. How else can we hope for real progress? If there is a taint of dependence anywhere it pollutes the whole of life's atmosphere. It may be that there are, as is said, physiological differences which make it impossible for men and women ever to be physically equal. But if there be one glory of the sun and another of the moon they are each equal within their own domain, and it is only by a recognition of this law of equality that a material universe is possible at all. In like manner it is only by recognising the perfect right of every human being to equal treatment because they are human beings that we can hope for better days for the race, and it is only when humanity, weary of the burden which Materialism has placed upon its bent and drooping shoulders, resolves to stand erect in the truth of a perfect equality, that it can hope to be saved from its self-imposed sorrow and suffering.

CHAPTER 7

FROM SERFDOM TO SOCIALISM

THE MODERN SOCIALIST movement is but a
continuation of the fight for freedom which
the disinherited have been waging since long
ere yet history carries any record of man's doings.
Sociology – a science still in its infancy – leaves us in
no doubt as to the process by which the mass of the
people have been brought under subjection to the few.
A nomadic herd of only partially developed human
beings barely one degree removed from the brute and
in which the family tie has not yet emerged, finally
settles on some favoured spot. In process of time it
becomes a settled community, owning all things in
common, and living mainly by the produce of the
chase. As experience develops intelligence, crude forms
of agriculture begin to make their appearance; certain
animals are domesticated, and the family tie is slowly
evolved. Property, hitherto confined to weapons of the
chase, usually buried with their owner, expands until
it includes the produce of some particular bit of soil,
and inheritance follows in the wake of its growth. By

this time the undisciplined horde has evolved some settled form of government, and is in a fair way to becoming prosperous. In the main it remains Communistic save in the matter of personal belongings, which may now include cattle. About this period, however, one of two things, sometimes both, usually happen which gradually changes the entire outlook for the little village commonwealth. Either a ruling caste is set up which acquires more and more control over the land from which all alike draw their sustenance until it finally succeeds in reducing the mass of the people to a condition of dependence upon its will, or some other and stronger tribe, regarding its neighbour's goods with covetous eye, invades and subdues and conquers the community, and reduces it to a state of bondage to its conquerors. For the sake of clearness I have reduced the process to its simplest form, and the reader has but to expand the illustration until the nation takes the place of the settlement to have a picture presented to his mind's eye of how in the earlier stages of progress man is brought into subjection to his fellow. Private property and war have been the great enslavers since man began to play his part in the world's history.

At a subsequent stage a new factor comes into play to still further complicate the situation. All settled nations tend in course of time to become traders as well as agriculturists. Beginning in barter and exchange among themselves and for their own convenience, the barter gradually expands until it becomes commerce with neighbouring and even far-distant peoples. A separate class of merchants come into being who trade for profit. Articles are no longer primarily made or grown for the use of the people themselves, but for sale and for export to other lands. By this means a second wealthy class is evolved, and capitalistic production for profit is set up. In the earlier stages of the world's history, and particularly in the Republics and Empires of the East, most of the work for the capitalist, as well as for the large land-owning class, was done by slaves. Prisoners of war, or poor people unable to pay their debts, were permitted to live on condition that they agreed to forfeit every human right. Even in the great free Republics of Greece and Rome nearly all the manual labour was done by nameless Helots who had no rights of any kind, were paid no wages, were in some cases flogged every day for offences which they might commit; might be put to death at the will of their master, were not permitted to know their own children, were placed even by great philosophers and reformers like Solon and Lycurgus on the same level as beasts without a soul, and were sometimes fed on food more offensive than that given to cattle. From time to time they broke out into open revolt, but were always reduced to subjection by the most merciless severity. As they multiplied rapidly, and as their masters were compensated for such as were killed in revolt, these uprisings were not always an unwelcome method of reducing their surplus numbers whilst putting public money in the pockets of their owners. When there were no risings the young bloods of the period were wont to thin them out by battues in much the same way as rookeries are kept down nowadays. As a result, work of any kind soon came to be considered too degrading for a citizen of the Republic to perform. Even the skilled artisans and artificers allowed their skill to pass into the hands of the slave class. Under such circumstances it is not to be wondered at that secret societies flourished, and that revolts were frequent, and that Rome's peril from the invader was looked upon by the slaves as their opportunity to press their claim for freedom. Patriotism is not a plant which thrives in the heart of the oppressed. But let it be noted that the slave's dream of freedom did not go beyond a desire to be free to sell his labour. Towards the end, and when the Republics of Greece, and latterly the Roman Empire, were tottering to their fall, a demand for political power began to make itself heard in the clamour for industrial freedom; but, in the main, what the slave conceived to be freedom did not go beyond the right to dispose of his labour to the highest bidder and to have some rights of property over his own person.

If the idea of freedom conceived by the Helot of antiquity had, when realised, been real freedom, then the modern worker should indeed be free. He has every right which his ancient forerunner was constantly risking his life to win for himself and his class. He is free to dispose of his labour when and how he can; free to come and free to go; free to combine and free to strike. He has all the rights of free citizenship in a free State which were enjoyed by the Patricians of the free Republics of ancient days. He has, in fact, all the outward attributes of freedom. And yet he is not free. A stern necessity compels him to give his toil for the benefit of a master just as the law compelled the slave two thousand years ago. The wages he receives for his free labour are often below the limit of bare subsistence. At the lower end of the modern industrial scale there are millions whose lot in life can be no better than was that of the average slave, and must be much worse than was that of those slaves who were owned by a moderately humane master. The slave-owner was under obligation to provide food and shelter of some kind for his human chattels, and would find it to be in his own interest, apart from humane motives altogether, to keep them in good physical condition. The free workman of to-day has to provide his own food and shelter out of such scanty pittance as he can extract from a labour market in a state of chronic overcrowding, the supply always exceeding the demand. The form of freedom for which the Helot longed and fought, and which his modern prototype has won, has proved to be Dead Sea fruit. To the eye of hope it seemed fair, but when put to the test of eating, it turns out to be ashes. In a word, the workman is finding out that he has but exchanged one form of serfdom for another, and that the necessity of hunger is an even more cruel scourge than was the thong of the Roman taskmaster.

There are, however, circumstances in favour of the modern worker which give him a great advantage over his prototype of bygone days. Having proved the hollowness of the kind of freedom for which the slave yearned, he is to that extent nearer the true solution of the problem of the ages. Every illusion dispelled is a milestone passed on the road towards liberty. The vision of freedom is an ever expanding conception of life and its possibilities. Its evolution, like that of every other growth, can only proceed by stages from the crude and the immature to the more and more perfected. The slave dreams of emancipation the emancipated workman of citizenship; the enfranchised citizen of Socialism, the Socialist of Communism. It is hopeless to expect that a people who are in the full enjoyment of political liberty will be content to continue for ever in a state of industrial servitude. Socialism represents the same principle in industry which Radicalism represented in politics – Equality. The workman who is a fully enfranchised Citizen of the State is a veritable Helot in the workshop. Obviously this state of things cannot go on for ever. He will use the political freedom which his fathers won for him to win industrial freedom for his children. That is the real inward meaning of the rise of the Labour party.

To this it may be retorted that the workman in his organised capacity as a trade unionist is able to regu-

late and control the terms and conditions of his
employment. This is true within limits in certain well-
organised trades, but to understand the full bearing of
the retort the limitations within which it is true require
to be carefully kept in mind. In fixing a rate of pay a
trade union can do a great deal, but it has little if any
control over the circumstances which in the final resort
decide the workman's earnings. In most of the skilled
trades and occupations the unions have succeeded in
fixing a standard rate of wages which is recognised by
the employers. In mining a certain Minimum wage
rate has been fixed, and no matter what the state of
trade the masters require to pay that minimum rate so
long as the agreement lasts. So far so good, but we
must look behind the wage agreement to learn the
helplessness of the workman. Take mining: so long as
the iron trades of the world are brisk there is a demand
for coal and the miner is fully employed, but when the
iron trade slackens the demand for coal falls off and
the miner goes upon short time. His minimum wage
may be honourably paid in terms of the contract for
the days on which he is employed, but he may only be
employed half time, an experience I regret to say only
too common in mining districts. He thus finds his
income cut down by one half, and his union is power-
less to do anything on his behalf. Neither he nor his
union had any hand in shaping the circumstances
which led to his being fully employed, nor has he or it
any control over those which cut his earnings down by

one half. He feels himself to be under the sway of forces which work quite without his ken, and which have the power to make him the victim of their caprice. Should he complain, he is told that the employer cannot be expected to keep the mines going at a loss since that would inflict an injury upon capital, and once again the workman finds himself up against something outwith himself. This capital which must not be injured is not his, he neither owns nor controls it, but its claims to consideration have priority over his. If he is of an inquiring turn of mind he may discover for himself that capital must be a plant of healthy growth, since in a single century it has increased its bulk to eighteen times its former size; that every improvement in machinery increases the earning power of capital without materially bettering his lot in life. It is a fact attested by the late Professor Thorold Rogers that whereas in the days of Henry III. – that is, some six hundred years ago – and ere yet a single power machine of any kind had been thought of, an agricultural labourer received wages which measured by the present-day standard of value were equal to £154 a year of our money, and a carpenter or mason £220, whereas now, when production of all kinds, save perhaps agriculture, has been increased an hundred-fold, the representatives of the same classes only receive £30 and £100 respectively. Further, it is indisputable that the tendency is for capital to congregate in an ever-lessening number of hands. Twelve families own one half of the whole area of Scotland. In the United States of America, where capitalism has reached its fullest development, *one per cent. of the population owns ninety-nine per cent. of the wealth.* Great Britain has not quite reached the same degree of wealth concentration, but the process is going on here also. During the first six years of this century forty-six persons died in Great Britain whose estates had an aggregate value of £78,000,000. During the sixteen years ending in 1906 no fewer than 750 separate trading firms in Great Britain merged themselves into fifty-one great Trusts, with a total capital of £170,000,000 sterling. The same process is going on in every industrial country. What we are witnessing now in trade and commerce is not the individual manufacturer or trader bidding for a reasonable share of the world's trade, but great masses of capital massed together like the forces of modern warfare, clashing and contending for supremacy with a force and shock which betimes shakes the world. In this Titanic conflict the small capitalist is pounded to powder by the clubs of the mighty giants of finance whilst the workman and his interests are too insignificant to be even remembered. Many of the modern Trusts already are, and most soon will be, international in their operations, and have a monopoly more or less of the article which they produce. Should the workpeople employed by the combine in any particular country prove refractory or show any inclination to rebel, the works there can be shut down for repairs for a month or six weeks, at the end of which time the refractory workers have been made tame enough by hunger. Meanwhile the orders are being supplied by working overtime in some other country where the Trust has works and the cost of the stoppage can be met by a very small increase in the cost to the consumer. This is no fanciful imaginary picture of what may happen, but a sober statement of what has already happened on several occasions and been threatened in several others. Clearly the Trade Union cannot stand up against forces so closely knit, so far-reaching and so omnipotent as those of the International Trust. The workman who sups daily in the presence of the gaunt wolf Poverty has to be careful lest it fall upon and devour him; the millionaire at the head of the Trust who can reckon upon an assured return of from fifty to one hundred per cent. upon his investments, which may mean from one million to five millions pounds a year for him, has no such fear. With hunger for an ally, he can afford to smile at his workman's discontent.

In another direction also the trade union falls short of meeting the circumstances of modern industry. I refer to the increasing evil of unemployment. In the best of times the average for the skilled trades is 3 per cent. out of work, rising to 8 per cent. in bad times. In certain trades connected with shipbuilding the percentage rises to over 14, and goes even higher in the unskilled occupations. The most which the trade union can do in these cases is to provide a small out-of-work benefit to tide the unfortunate member over until trade again takes a turn for the better. When 5 per cent. of the skilled artisans are out of work it is a safe assumption that a much larger proportion are only working short time. Here obviously nothing that the workman can do can be of much avail; there is no "demand" for his labour, and so there is nothing for it but to kill time as best he may until a "demand" arises. To use Carlyle's figure he, like long-eared Midas, is reduced to the point of starvation surrounded by the wealth which his own touch has called into being. There is surplus food and raiment and fuel stored up all around him, and he is suffering from lack of all three, but, like the victim of some uncanny spell, he cannot reach that which he most needs. Tantalus must have been intended to represent the strong clever willing man out of work and starving in the midst of plenty.

Such are some of the more outstanding features of modern industrialism for which the workman hitherto has been unable to find a remedy, for which he has been expressly and explicitly told by his political and economic guides there can be no remedy but only palliatives. Hitherto he has believed them, and gone on suffering and enduring as best he might. Now he is beginning to see that were he master and owner of capital and of land he would no longer be at the mercy of a blind bloodless force outside himself which at present he cannot control, and he thinks of using the State to aid him in acquiring this mastery and ownership. Herein we have the beginning of conscious Socialism.

This generation has grown up ignorant of the fact that Socialism is as old as the race and has never been without its witness. Ere civilisation dawned upon the world, primitive man was living his rude Communistic life, sharing all things in common with every member of his tribe or gens and bringing forth the rudiments of the emotional, the ethical and the artistic faculties. Later when the race lived in villages and ere yet towns or cities had been built, Man, the Communist, moved about among the communal flocks and herds on communal land. The peoples who have carved their names most deeply on the tables of human story all set out on their conquering career as Communists, and their downward path begins with the day when they finally turned away from it and began to gather personal possessions. Every popular movement of the past seven hundred years has been a Socialist movement at bottom. The peasants on the Continent of Europe were, as we have already seen, first fired to enter upon their thirty years' war by Communists; the peasants' revolt in England was led by a Communist; in the struggle against the divine right of kings, which ended in the establishment of the Cromwellian Commonwealth, a strong Communist sect strove mightily to make Communism the policy of the new order. Liberty, Equality, Fraternity was the slogan which roused the people of France to their mighty effort for freedom. The towns which made great the name of Italy were communal, as were also the towns of England in the days of their power. When the old civilisations were putrefying, the still small voice of Jesus the Communist stole over the earth like a soft refreshing breeze carrying healing wherever it went. When Capitalism was in process of converting England into a veritable hell, it was Robert Owen the Communist who gave his fortune and his life in an effort to save her people from destruction. When the hell had been made and the Chartist movement was in full swing, its leaders were Socialists almost to a man, as had been those of the Radical movement before them. It was fear of Socialism much more than of Radicalism which led to the Peterloo massacre. When Radicalism with its arid gospel of selfishness was blatant with the joy of triumph, the imposing form of William Morris the Communist stood lonely and grand like a beacon on a mighty rock in the midst of a storm-tossed sea warning the people of England of the danger towards which they were heading. So that it may truly be said of Socialism that in no period of the world's history has it been without its witness, nor has there ever been any rising of the people which was not enthused and inspired by its principles. And now, in the International Socialist movement we are at last in the presence of a force which is gathering unto itself the Rebel spirits of all lands and uniting them into a mighty host to do battle, not for the triumph of a sect, or of a race, but for the overthrow of a system which has filled the world with want and woe. Workers of the world unite, wrote Karl Marx; you have a world to win, and nothing to lose but your chains. And they are uniting under the crimson banner of a world-embracing principle which knows nor sect, nor creed, nor race, and which offers new life and hope to all created beings – the glorious Gospel of Socialism.

CHAPTER 8

SUMMARY AND CONCLUSION

F ROM AMOEBA TO Man there has been a steady and more or less continuous progress. Some power has been at work seeking to make life perfect; sometimes acting through the pressure of hard circumstance, at others weaning life onwards to new heights of development; now bringing forth the tooth and claw, and, anon, the wondrous mother-love. Evolution may explain the process which has been at work; it does not explain the motive power which set the process in motion. That still remains hidden from our ken, but that it exists is no longer denied by even the most materialistic of our scientists. There must be some principle of beauty and perfection in the Universe towards which all creation is reaching out and seeking to attain. How otherwise account for the wealth of beauty of form and colour which everywhere meets the eye? To say that all the charm, all the sweet and holy influence of Nature, is the product of blind material-istic unguided force is, to me at least, unthinkable. I cannot bring myself to admit that hatred, hunger, and fear have been the only, or even the greatest, factors in the evolution of love and the moral faculties. Dead matter must have remained dead matter for all time had not the spirit of life been breathed into it. Whence came it? Not from matter, for that is lifeless. And so I claim that the Socialist, even when working as he necessarily does at present mainly, though not by any means altogether, in the realm of material things, is the human agent consciously co-operating with that great principle of growth and development which, for lack of a better term, we call the Divine Life, and assisting it to find higher and fuller expression in the human race. And this same spirit of progress will continue at work under Socialism, only at a greatly accelerated pace. Combination and Co-operation, not Individualism and Competition, are the means by which progress from the lower to the higher forms of life is achieved, a fact now admitted by all leading scientists and naturalists, and by none more so than by Darwin himself. If Socialism meant, as its opponents say it would, stagnation, then it would fail, and the Socialist State would have to give way to one more adapted to the needs of the race. There can be no finality, even in Socialism. There is no thing over which *finis* is written anywhere in life. Either we are going forward or we are being driven back. There is no such thing as standing still. Movement and change are of the very essence of life. Socialism we believe to be the next step in the evolution of that form of State which will give the individual the fullest and freest room for expansion and development. State Socialism, with all its drawbacks, and these I frankly admit, will prepare the way for free Communism in which the rule, not merely the law of the State, but the rule of life will be – From each according to his ability, to each according to his needs. Great philanthropic agencies, so much belauded by anti-Socialists, are but the promise of these better times. The same spirit which leads the philanthropist to give time and money for the amelioration of the lot of the poor will, in the days to come when it is more developed, lead the same type of person to spend their strength and to find their highest good in ministering to the needs of the commonweal. Change of some kind there must be in our Social and Industrial Economy. A Communistic spirit germinates in people herded together in cities, massed together in factories, and thus made to feel a oneness of interest in their Civic and industrial relationship.

But whilst this is so, our form of property-owning remains individualistic. When property was widely distributed and all possessed some, the fact of it being privately owned was a small matter and one from which no great harm accrued. Now when land is held in the form of large estates and capital in great masses, the result is the oppression of the people. Whilst everything else has changed, the form in which property is held has remained stationary. It is this fact which explains why our Civilisation rests on a Helot class which is compelled to give its whole time and talent to the owners of property in exchange for a precarious supply of the barest necessaries of life, and whose greatest concern is where the next meal is to come from. It is this condition of things which Socialism proposes to remedy.

If, as Herbert Spencer said, life means internal correspondence to external environment, then Socialism or decay are the alternatives we have to face. What we have at present is an altruistic spirit struggling against an individualistic environment. The change which the Socialist seeks is to make the material environment correspond to the ethical spirit. Progress cannot for ever be confined by the cerements of a dead past. Unless the Social quagmire of Poverty can be cleansed, its foul miasma will poison the blood of the body politic and produce decay and death.

We have seen how in our own country the boundaries of freedom have been widening with the progress of the ages. The slave of a thousand years ago, with no more right than the swine he tended, has fought his way upward through Serfdom to Citizenship. The modern workman is theoretically the equal in the eye of the law of every other class. His vote carries equal weight in the ballot box with that of the millionaire who employs him; he is as free to worship when and how he pleases as the noblest baron; his rights are in all respects the same as theirs. Combination and energy have raised him to where he now stands. But his task is

James Keir Hardie, in 1902, pictured on the steps of his rustic
summer house, at Lochnorris, with his pet dog, Roy (ILP/WCML).

Hardie's home at Lochnorris, Cumnock, from a souvenir postcard issued in 1910. The house was built for him and his family in 1891, overlooking both the main road into town and one of Robert Burns' favourite streams (ILP/WCML).

The young Keir Hardie: miner, temperance activist and avid reader of Burns and Carlyle. The first known photograph of Hardie, taken in Glasgow in 1872, when he was just sixteen (by permission of East Ayrshire Leisure/East Ayrshire Council).

faithfully yours
J Keir Hardie

A signed photo of Keir Hardie in his workingman's
cap. The portrait, which served as part of Hardie's self-
definition, was taken as a publicity shot for his West
Ham election campaign in 1892 (by permission of East
Ayrshire Leisure/East Ayrshire Council).

New Year's Card for 1903, sent to Hardie by John Bruce Glasier. Socialism is set fair to deliver for both the old and young in Scotland (by permission of East Ayrshire Leisure/East Ayrshire Council).

All 29 Labour MPs are pictured on the terrace at Westminster after the electoral triumph of 1906. Keir Hardie sits squarely at the centre of the group, flanked by Arthur Henderson and David Shackleton. Ramsay MacDonald is seated third from the left.

Philip Snowden broods on the very back row (9th from right);
while James O'Grady of the Cabinet Makers and Will Thorne of
the Gas Workers establish a firm presence standing on the right
edge of the picture (ILP/WCML).

Keir Hardie pictured in Perth, Western Australia, at the
height of his 'World Tour' in 1907 (ILP/WCML).

A Certificate of Suffragette Support owned by Keir Hardie, and signed by Emmeline Pankhurst (by permission of East Ayrshire Leisure/East Ayrshire Council).

The campaigner for Women's Suffrage: Keir Hardie speaking on the plinth of Nelson's Column, Trafalgar Square, 19 May 1906. Emmeline Pankhurst stands behind him, Charlotte Despard is at the back (ILP/WCML).

The campaigner for Labour: Keir Hardie in his Merthyr constituency during the General Election of 1910. Canvassing with him are Charlotte Bernard Shaw, the Reverend Geoffrey Ramsay and George Bernard Shaw. The worlds of religion, the arts and politics combine for the Labour cause (ILP/WCML).

International Solidarity: Keir Hardie shaking hands with
Jean Jaures, the great French Socialist leader (ILP/WCML).

Among the people: Hardie campaigning in the Forest of Dean, in 1912 (ILP/WCML).

The human touch: Keir Hardie presented with a flower by the youngest member of the audience, c.1914 (ILP/WCML).

Hardie's aim was to unite the political and industrial arms of the British Labour Movement. At the height of the General Strike, in 1926, the leaders of the Chopwell miners, in County Durham rallied around a banner portraying Hardie as one of the central figures guiding international Socialism (Tom Sawyer Collection).

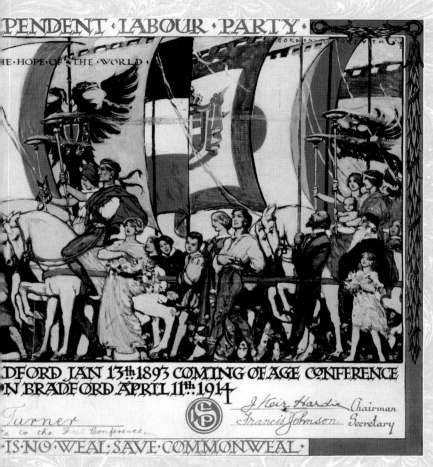

Certificate for the Independent Labour Party's 'Coming of Age Conference', held in Bradford on 11 April 1914, and signed by Keir Hardie. Labour marches forward under the flags of all nations. Yet within four months this fraternity would be swept aside by the outbreak of the war that would break Keir Hardie's heart (by permission of the People's History Museum).

Keir Hardie the
journalist and author,
in his London flat at
Neville's Court, pencil
firmly tucked behind
his ear (ILP/WCML).

Front cover of the first
edition of *From Serfdom to
Socialism*, published in 1907.

not yet finished; the long drawn out struggle is not yet over. There is one more battle to be fought, one more fortress to be assailed ere he stands within the charmed circle of perfect equality. He has yet to overcome property and win economic freedom. When he has made property his servant, not his master, he will literally have put all his enemies under his feet. He will also have proved his fitness to survive as being the best fitted to live. He is better equipped for the struggle than ever were any of those who have gone before. Each position won has been a vantage ground from which to conduct the next onslaught.

Darwinism, with its creed of a pitiless struggle for existence in which the scrupulous were trampled out of life, harmonised completely with, and for a time appeared to give new life to, the Manchester School of Economics, whose conception of Society as a heartless mass of warring units, each intent upon the destruction of its neighbour, had led to results quite as appalling as those depicted by Darwin in the lower realms of life: the public conscience was beginning to revolt against an order of things which seemed so inhuman when Darwin stepped to the front with a theory which seemed to justify every cruelty as being part of the price which had to be paid for progress. It was in the early eighties that what came to be known as Darwinism thus gave a fillip to the competitive system by appearing to stamp it with the sign manual of scientific approval. The doctrine of the struggle for existence and survival of the fittest was eagerly s'eized hold of and put to uses for which the writings of Darwin himself gave no sanction. His tentative statements and deductions from the facts of life, as he saw them, were hailed as *ex cathedra* utterances from which there could be no appeal. Because hunger appeared to be the spur which led the lower forms of life to struggle and compete with each other for subsistence, therefore, it was argued, it was necessary to retain hunger as the spur wherewith to keep mankind on the move. The struggle for existence was emphasised as though it were the whole law of life. The greater fact that life did not depend upon struggle but upon adaptation to environment, was lightly slurred over. The Darwinian apologists for Capitalism made little if any reference to the fact that no matter how fierce the struggle, life could not be kept alive unless it could be made to harmonise with its environment. They tried to conceal the fact that the survival of the fittest only meant, and was only intended to mean, that that form of life flourished and survived best which was most in harmony with its surroundings; and that the fittest did not necessarily mean the best, but only those best equipped for the conditions in which they found themselves. Now it is seen that neither the doctrine of the struggle for existence nor that of the survival of the fittest lends the slightest countenance to modern industrial conditions. In nature bird and beast are free to seek and take food and shelter wherever these are to be found; in modern Society man must find some one to give him work wherewith he may earn wages before he is entitled to either food or shelter, and before this one fact the whole arguments so laboriously built up by the so-called Darwinists falls to pieces. Darwin stated emphatically that "those communities which included the greatest number of the most *sympathetic* members would flourish best," and in so stating he conceded the whole case for which the Socialist is contending. It is sympathetic association and not individualistic competition which makes for progress and the improvement of the race.

Letourneau tells us that the ambition of the very earliest man was to eat and not to be eaten. The issue does not seem to have changed much in the millions of years which have elapsed since this was the victory song of the successful combatant. The next issue probably was to kill and not to be killed, followed by to enslave and not to be enslaved. To-day it takes no higher form than to cheat and not to be cheated. That, however, cannot be the last word in the vocabulary of progress. Surely it is reasonable to hope that a day will dawn in which a desire to serve rather than to be served shall be the spur which shall drive men onward to noble deeds.

Whatever differences there may be in the International Socialist Movement concerning the tactics to be pursued in achieving Socialism, there is perfect agreement on two leading points of principle: hostility to

Militarism in all its forms and to war as a method of settling disputes between nations is the first. In countries where the Socialist parties are a real influence in the councils of the nation, the war spirit is suffering appreciable eclipse. It would, for instance, be a difficult task, and one yearly becoming more so, for the rulers of say France and Germany, to again embroil these two nations in war with each other. Probably the first effective service to which the growing forces of International Socialism will be put will be to make war upon war. The Holy Alliance which Socialism is achieving is not that of crowned heads but of horny hands, and therein lies the only real hope there is of peace on earth. The other point of agreement concerns the essential principle of Socialism. In one form or another public must be substituted for private ownership and control of land and capital. Whether this result is to be attained by State Socialism, or by free voluntary association, like our Cooperative movement, or, as seems most likely, a combination of both, is a point upon which a healthy difference of opinion may well exist; but the difference concerns the method to be employed, not the end itself, upon which all are agreed, viz., that the useful classes must own the tools wherewith they labour and be free to enjoy the full produce resulting from their labour.

To dogmatise about the form which the Socialist State shall take is to play the fool. That is a matter with which we have nothing whatever to do. It belongs to the future, and is a matter which posterity alone can decide. The most we can hope to do is to make the coming of Socialism possible in the full assurance that it will shape itself aright when it does come. We have seen how mankind when left free has always and in all parts of the world naturally turned to Communism. That it will do so again is the most likely forecast of the future which can be made, and the great industrial organisations, the Trades Unions, the Co-operative Movement, the Friendly Orders, the Socialist Organisations and the Labour Party are each and all developing the feeling of solidarity and of mutual aid which will make the inauguration of Communism a comparatively easy task as the natural successor to State Socialism.

As for progress and development under Socialism, these may be safely left to care for themselves. What necessity does for the lower orders of creation, man's reasoning powers will be equal to accomplishing for the highest. Already we have abundant testimony to support this point of view. It would probably take Nature, unaided by man, a thousand years, working along the lines of necessity and natural selection, to so improve the breed of cattle as to increase the yield of milk per cow from 526 to 826 gallons a year, the larger yield being of better quality and costing no more to produce than the smaller. This, however, is what Mr. John Speir, a well-known cattle breeder, has succeeded in doing in his own lifetime.

The average yield of wheat in Great Britain is 28

bushels to the acre sown. Experiments at Rothamstead show that 38 bushels can be got quite as easily if only the proper methods be adopted, whilst on allotment farms the yield is from 40 to 57 bushels per acre. One single grain of barley planted by Major Hallett near Brighton, the result of crossing and selection, yielded 110 separate ears containing from 5000 to 6000 grains. An ordinary barley stalk only carries from two to four ears carrying about 65 grains each. Similar experiments obtained equally remarkable results from wheat. Again, the average yield of potatoes is 6 tons to the acre, but by crossing and transplanting already a yield of 34 tons 9 cwt. has been realised in Great Britain. These illustrations of what man can do in the way of assisting Nature could be multiplied *ad infinitum*. The struggle of the future will be for improvement on the moral plane, and competition of the kind we are now familiar with is fatal to progress in the higher realms of development. It is only when the material things of life find easy and abundant satisfaction that the higher powers come into play.

The reward of genius under Socialism cannot well be less than it has been under Commercialism. Most men of genius die poor, a fair proportion of them die of hunger, unless they commit suicide in time. Genius has always been its own reward. The one thing the Genius asks is to be left free to give expression to the thoughts that burn in his overtaxed brain. No really great Genius ever was a business man or ever could be.

Most of the world's most priceless treasures in literature and art have been the work of men who, like the perfectly happy man of the Eastern fable, were shirtless. The inventor falls into a different class from the genius, but he too invents for invention's sake. He invents because he cannot help inventing and too often the reward of his invention goes to others. Under Socialism the inventor would be a much more honoured person than he is now. Mechanical invention under Capitalism has as its first and most direct outcome the dismissal of numbers of men and women who would otherwise have been kept employed. John Stuart Mill, it will be remembered, questioned whether mechanical invention had lightened the labours of a single human being. An invention may cheapen the cost of the article produced and thus benefit the consumer, but often a terrible price has to be paid in human suffering. Under Socialism, when machinery is socially owned, every invention will benefit producer and consumer alike – the former by lightening the burden of his toil, and the latter by reducing the cost of living. The Socialist State, therefore, will have good reason to honour the inventor, and will have a direct interest in rewarding him as a public benefactor.

A like reasoning applies to the argument that under Socialism, the spur of necessity being removed, there would be an all-round tendency to shirk work and that production would thus be lessened and poverty be as rife then as now. But surely this is to argue against all we know of poor maligned human nature. To begin with, the weary round, the thankless task of present-day drudgery could under Socialism be reduced by two-thirds and still leave the resources of the nation equal to what they are at present. On the most moderate estimate that can be framed, two-thirds is the proportion of the national income which is now paid in rent and interest to the owners of land and capital. Whole armies of men and women are now kept at work on tasks which, under Socialism, would no longer be necessary. Let those who doubt this think of the numbers who are engaged as clerks and the like, of the members of the Stock Exchange, of the multiplication of small struggling shopkeepers, of the commercial travellers, of domestic servants of both sexes who pander to the vicious tastes and luxurious habits of the idle rich, of the numbers unemployed and of those only partially employed (I say nothing for the moment of the Naval and Military Services of the Crown). Imagine all these set free from the non-productive work which now occupies them, or the no work as the case may be, and merged in the army employed in useful production. Their maintenance would cost no more then than it does now, and each would be producing more than enough to provide for their own maintenance. With land and machinery socially owned, with the parasites wiped out, with the entire nation organised so as to turn each individual's service to the most profitable account, work would become a mere incident in a man's life instead of being the all-engrossing thing it is to-day.

And as the workers would be working for themselves, each would have an interest in producing everything of the best and seeing not only that every one else did the same but that no one shirked his share of the work to be done. The healthy human being likes congenial work. It is only when it is toilsome task-work in which he has neither personal interest nor pride of acknowledgment that shirking is practised.

My task is at an end. I have sought to present Socialism from the human – the visionary point of view if the reader will have it so. As one writer has well said: If anything is to be really done in this world it must be done by Visionaries, by men who see the future, and make the future because they see it. The inventor and discoverer must see with the eye of faith the thing he wants to accomplish before it takes form and shape to the eye of flesh. I have not sought to theorise or philosophise. Most of our differences are due to verbal theorisings which homely common sense puts to rout in the everyday experience of life.

The simple nameless herd of Humanity
Hath deeds and faith that are truth enough for me!

I have not sought to shirk or gloss over the difficulties of my subject. The one thing I ask is that difficulties concerning matters of detail which have not arisen shall not be allowed to stand in the way of the acceptance of the principles which Socialism represents. Everything has had to grow; the State as we know it is the growth of thousands of years Electricity, the post-office, the railway system, machinery, have all grown from small beginnings to the wonderful things we now see them. With each new necessity a new development has been forthcoming. So too with Socialism. Once the principle has been accepted, then experience and common sense will find the way to overcome every difficulty which may arise in connection with its working.

We cannot go on as we are. Nemesis is one of the grim realities not sufficiently taken into account in the great game of life. Leaden-footed she may be, and often is, but that is only her merciful way of giving the sinner time to repent. There is nothing more certain in the Universe than that an injustice done to an individual, or to a class, or to a sex, or to a nation, will, if persisted in, sooner or later bring destruction upon the doer. Often too, in fact usually, the party to whom the wrong is done is the instrument used to bring about the overthrow of the wrongdoer. It was not the barbarians who overthrew the greatness of the Roman Empire. The greatness had already departed ere the Huns and Goths swept down upon its gates. Rome in her pristine strength would have rolled back her invaders as a rock returns the onslaught of an angry sea. Ill-gotten wealth and debauchery had corrupted the early patriotism of the Roman Patrician, and idle dependence upon the largesse of the rich had destroyed the vigour of the Plebeians, so that when the barbarians thundered at the gates of the Eternal City there was no force of manhood within to deny them entrance. History is one long record of like illustrations.

Must our modern civilisation with all its teeming wonders come to a like end? We are reproducing in faithful detail every cause which led to the downfall of the civilisations of other days – Imperialism, taking tribute from conquered races, the accumulation of great fortunes, the development of a population which owns no property, and is always in poverty. Land has gone out of cultivation and physical deterioration is an alarming fact. And so we Socialists say the system which is producing these results must not be allowed to continue. A system which has robbed religion of its savour, destroyed handicraft, which awards the palm of success to the unscrupulous, corrupts the press, turns pure women on to the streets, and upright men into mean-spirited time-servers, cannot continue. In the end it is bound to work its own overthrow. Socialism with its promise of freedom, its larger hope for humanity, its triumph of peace over war, its binding of the races of the earth into one all-embracing brotherhood, must prevail. Capitalism is the creed of the dying present; Socialism throbs with the life of the days that are to be. It has claimed its martyrs in the past, is claiming them now, will claim them still; but what then? Better to

Rebel and die in twenty worlds
Sooner than bear the yoke of thwarted life.

And let the final word also be George Eliot's in the form of an appeal to those who are hesitating:-

Nay, never falter, no great deed is done
By falterers who ask for certainty.
No good is certain but the steadfast mind,
The undivided will to seek the good;
'Tis that compels the elements, and wrings
A human music from the indifferent air.
The greatest gift the hero leaves his race
Is to have been a hero. Say we fail!
We feed the high tradition of the world
And leave our spirits in our children's breasts.

APPENDIX

Consisting of Quotations from Eminent Authorities, and intended to illustrate some of the main issues raised by the Author.

CHAPTER 1

SOCIALISM AND COMMUNISM, SOME DEFINITIONS

What is characteristic of Socialism is the joint ownership by all the members of the community of the instruments and means of production, which carries with it the consequence that the division of all the produce among the body of owners must be a public act performed according to the rules laid down by the community.

—JOHN STUART MILL, *Philosopher and Political Economist.*

Whereas industry is at the present carried on by private capitalists served by wage labour, it must be in future conducted by associated or co-operating workmen jointly owning the means of production. On grounds both of theory and history this must be accepted as the cardinal principle of Socialism.

—*Encyclopaedia Britannica.*

The Alpha and Omega of Socialism is the transformation of private and competing capitals into a united collective capital.

—Professor SCHAFFLE, Author of the
Quintessence of Socialism.

The result of the analysis of Socialism may be brought together in a definition which would read somewhat as follows: Socialism is that contemplated system of industrial society which proposes the abolition of private property in the great material instruments of production, and the substitution therefor of collective property; and advocates the collective management of production, together with the distribution of social income by society and private property in the larger proportion of this social income.

—Professor R.T. ELY, Author of
Socialism and Social Reform.

Communism is the theory which teaches that the labour and the income of society should be distributed equally among all its members by some constituted authority.

—Palgrave's *Dictionary of Political Economy.*

Socialism: Any system of social organisation which would abolish entirely, or in great part, the individual effort and competition on which modern society rests, and substitute co-operation, would introduce a more perfect and equal distribution of the products of labour, and would make land and capital, as the instruments of production, the joint possession of the members of the community.

—The *Century Dictionary*.

Socialism: The abolition of that individual action on which modern societies depend, and the substitution of a regulated system of co-operative action.

—The *Popular Encyclopedia*.

Socialism A theory of society which advocates a more precise, orderly, and harmonious arrangement of the social relations of mankind than that which has hitherto prevailed.

—*Webster's Dictionary*.

Socialism: The science of reconstructing society on an entirely new basis, by substituting the principles of association for that of competition in every branch of human industry.

—*Worcester's Dictionary*.

Socialism: A theory of civil polity that aims to secure the reconstruction of society, increase of wealth, and a more equal distribution of the products of labour through the public collective ownership of land and capital (as distinguished from property) and the public collective management of all industries. Its motto is: "Every one according to his need."

—*Standard Dictionary.*

Socialism, as understood by the Fabian Society, means the organisation and conduct of the necessary industries of the country, and the appropriation of all forms of economic rent of the land and capital, by the nation as a whole through the most suitable public authorities, parochial, municipal, provincial, or central.

—*Fabian Society,* London.

Socialism is that mode of social life which, based upon the recognition of the natural brotherhood and unity of mankind, would have land and capital owned by the community collectively, and operated co-operatively for the equal good of all.

—*American Fabian Society.*

Our aim, one and all, is to obtain for the whole community complete ownership and control of the means of transport, the means of manufacture, the mines and the land. Thus we look to put an end for ever to the wage system, to sweep away all distinctions of class, and eventually to establish national and international Communism on a sound basis.

—*Joint Manifesto,* British Socialist Bodies.

OBJECT: The Socialisation of the Means of Production, Distribution and Exchange, to be controlled by a Democratic State in the interests of the entire community, and the complete Emancipation of Labour from the Domination of Capitalism and Landlordism, with the establishment of Social and Economic Equality between the Sexes.

—Social Democratic Federation.

OBJECT: An Industrial Commonwealth founded upon the Socialisation of Land and Capital.

PROGRAM: The true object of industry being the production of the requirements of life, the responsibility should rest with the community collectively, therefore:

The land being the storehouse of all the necessaries of life should be declared and treated as public property.

The capital necessary for industrial operations should be owned and used collectively.

Work and wealth resulting therefrom should be equitably distributed over the population.

—Independent Labour Party.

CHAPTER 2

What capital does for production is to afford the shelter, protection, tools, and materials which the work requires, and to feed and otherwise maintain the labourers during the process. Whatever things are destined for this use, destined to supply productive labour with these various prerequisites, are capital.

—J. S. MILL.

Equity does not permit property in land. For if one portion of the earth's surface may justly become the possession of an individual, and may be held by him for his sole use and benefit, as a thing to which he has an exclusive right, then *other* portions of the earth's surface may be so held; and eventually the *whole* of the earth's surface may be so held; and our planet may thus altogether lapse into private hands. Observe now the dilemma to which this leads. Supposing the entire habitable globe to be so enclosed, it follows that if the land-owners have a valid right to its surface, all who are not land-owners have no right at all to its surface. Hence such can exist on the earth by sufferance only. They are all trespassers. Save by the permission of the lords of the soil, they can have no room for the soles of their feet. Nay, should the others think fit to deny them a resting-place, these landless men might equitably be expelled from the earth altogether.

—HERBERT SPENCER.

Socialism is one of the unforeseen results of the great industrial revolution of the past 150 years. During this period man's power over the rest of nature has suddenly and largely increased; new means of accumulating wealth, and also new means of utilising land and capital, have come into being. At the beginning of the last century, the whole value of the land and capital of England is estimated to have amounted to less than £500,000,000 sterling; now it is supposed to be over £9,000,000,000, an increase eighteen-fold. Two hundred years ago, rent and interest cannot have amounted to £30,000,000 sterling annually; now they absorb over £450,000,000. Socialism arose as soon as rent and interest became important factors.

—SIDNEY WEBB, Author of *Industrial Democracy*, &c.

The mechanical industries of the United States are carried on by steam and water-power, representing in round numbers, 3,500,000 horse-power, each horse-power equalling the muscular labour of six men; that is to say, if men were employed to furnish the power to carry on the industries of the country it would require 21,000,000 men, and 21,000,000 representing a population, according to the ratio of the census of 1880, of 105,000,000. The industries are now carried on by 4,000,000 persons in round numbers, representing a population of 20,000,000 only.

—Commissioner WRIGHT, *United States Bureau of Labour* (1886).

Let us not go further without a vision and a hope. That vision, that hope, is not of a regimented society, but of a community relieved from nine-tenths of its present irksome routine and carking care. If the individual is to be set free, it can only be in a society so organised as to reduce the labour employed in the production of common necessaries to a minimum. That minimum cannot be secured without the organisation of each of the great branches of production and distribution. Common needs can be satisfied with little labour if labour be properly applied. The work of a few will feed a hundred or supply exquisite cloth for the clothing of fifty. `The work for a few hours per day of every adult member of the community will be ample to supply every comfort in each season to all. Thus set free, the lives of men will turn to the uplifting, individual work which is the pride of the craftsman. The dwellings of men will contain not only the socialised products within common reach, but the proud individual achievements of their inmates. The simple and beautiful clothing of the community will chiefly be made of fabrics woven in the socialised factories, but it will often be worked by the loving hands of women. A happy union of labour economised in routine work and labour lavished upon individual work will uplift the crafts of the future and the character of those who follow them. The abominations of machine-made ornament will disappear, and art be wedded to every-day life

—L. G. CHIOZZA MONEY, M.P., Author of
Riches and Poverty.

CHAPTER 3

We have not now to deal with mere abstract and transcendental theories, but with a clearly defined movement in practical politics, appealing to some of the deepest instincts of a large proportion of the voting population, and professing to provide a program likely in the future to stand more and more on its own merits in opposition to all other programs whatever.

—BENJAMIN KIDD, Author of *Social Evolution,* &c.

But the above [figures showing the productivity of land], will be enough to caution the reader against hasty conclusions as to the impossibility of feeding 39,000,000 people from 78,000,000 acres. They also will enable me to draw the following conclusions:

(I) If the soil of the United Kingdom were cultivated only as it was thirty-five years ago, 24,000,000 people instead of 17,000,000 could live on home grown food, and that culture, while giving occupation to an additional 750,000 men, would give nearly 3,000,000 wealthy home customers to the British manufactures. (2) If the cultivable area in the United Kingdom were cultivated as the soil is cultivated on the average in Belgium, the United Kingdom would have food for at least 37,000,000 inhabitants; and it might export agricultural produce without ceasing to manufacture so as freely to supply all the needs of a wealthy population. And finally, (3), if the population of this country came to be doubled, all that would be required for producing the food for 80,000,000 inhabitants would be to cultivate the soil as it is cultivated in the best farms of this country, in Lombardy, and in Flanders, and to utilise some meadows, which at present lie almost unproductive, in the same way as the neighbourhoods of the big cities in France are utilised for market gardening. All these are not fancy dreams, but mere realities; nothing but modest conclusions from what we see round about us, without any allusion to the agriculture of the future.

—P. KROPOTKIN, Author of *Fields, Factories, and Workshops; Mutual Aid,* &c.

It cannot be too loudly proclaimed: economic evolution necessarily goes hand in hand with a moral development strictly related to it. Nowadays, broken into the individualistic system, we regard with astonishment the fierce patriotism which inflamed the little cities and republics of antiquity. But this sentiment was inspired by the very instinct of preservation. In the bosom of the clans and of the families interests were solid. Defeat might bring with it not only complete ruin, but also slavery. Patriotic enthusiasm was but the idealised love of property. As economic individualism progressed, the masses became detached from a *res publica* which no longer had anything public about it. The wealthy, the ruling classes, thought chiefly of maintaining and increasing their estates. As to the enslaved masses, what did a change of masters signify to them? "It is absurd," says Diodorus Siculus, speaking of Egypt, "to entrust the defence of a country to people who own nothing in it." This is a very wise reflection, and it is applicable not only to the people of antiquity ... The words on this occasion put into the mouth of Gracchus by Plutarch are forcible and even suggestive. He said, according to the chronicler, "that the wild beasts in Italy had at least their lairs, dens, and caves whereto they might retreat; whereas the men who fought and died for that land, had nothing in it save air and light, but were forced to wander to and fro with their wives and children, without resting-place or house, wherein they might lodge." ... The poor folk go forth to war to fight, and die for the delights, riches, and superfluities of others, and they are falsely called lords and rulers of the habitable world in that land where they have not so much as a single inch that they may call their own.

Everywhere in Greece plutocracy held sway, and all at once Hellenic patriotism, that formerly had been made so fiercely keen, disappeared. The preservation of their wealth became the chief care of the ruling classes, who nearly always made common cause with the foreign invaders. During the Peloponnesian war the populace took the part of the Athenians, the rich that of the Spartans. Likewise, during the Macedonian invasion, the rich – the "optimates" – were in favour of Philip of Macedon. Finally, later on, when the Roman legions appeared, the aristocrats again made terms with the invaders.

It was much worse at Athens, a maritime city of commerce and manufacture, a kind of Hellenic England where stock-jobbing, usury, and financial speculations were rampant; where the body social was divided into two inimical classes – a minority having in their grasp the greater part of the capital, which it was their constant anxiety to increase, and a proletarian populace, of necessity hostile to the moneyed aristocracy. The sequel is known, character became demoralised; the ancient and heroic ancestral virtues faded away; the ruling classes subordinated the city's interests to those of their strong boxes; Philip came on the scene unexpectedly. There always comes a Philip to subjugate degenerate Athenians. Then to the brilliant flash of Alexander's conquests succeeded political despotism, and in the end Greece, the glorious, became only a Roman province ... Finally, in the last days of Independent Greece, and afterwards in Imperial Rome, a condition of striking social inequality existed. On one side a small minority held the greater part of wealth; on the other was an enslaved and degraded crowd. The first usually inclined to subordinate the general interests to their own particular interests, cared nothing for the common country, which for the rest was no longer common; the others, the disinherited, had nothing to defend, and at most ran no other risk than that of changing masters. The conqueror, barbarous or not, could not fail to appear; he intervened always whenever great wealth was amassed in the hands of a population incapable of defending it.

—CH. LETOURNEAU, Author of
Property: Its Origin and Development.

If this were the real state of things, England would be a perfect paradise for working men! If every man, woman, and child returned as a worker in the census had full employment, at full wages, for forty-eight weeks out of the fifty-two, there would be no poverty at all. We should be in the millennium! Far other is the real state of affairs; and a very different tale would be told by scores and even hundreds of thousands, congregated in our large cities, and seeking in vain for sufficient work.

None but those who have examined the facts can have any idea of the precariousness of employment in our large cities, and the large proportion of time out of work, and also, I am bound to add, the loss of time in many well-paid trades from drinking habits. Taking all these facts into account, I come to the conclusion, that for loss of work from every cause, and for the non-effectives up to sixty-five years of age, who are included in the census, we ought to deduct fully twenty per cent. from the nominal full-time wages.

—DUDLEY BAXTER, Author of
The National Income, &c.

CHAPTER 4

The soil was given to rich and poor in common. Wherefore, oh ye rich! do you unjustly claim it for yourselves alone?... Nature gave all things in common for the use of all, usurpation created private right.

—ST. AMBROSE.

Behold, the idea we should have of the rich and covetous they are truly as robbers, who, standing in the public highways, despoil the passers-by; they who convert their chambers into caverns, in which they bury the goods of others.

—ST. JOHN CHRYSOSTOM.

It is no great thing not to rob others of their belongings, and in vain do they think themselves innocent who appropriate to their own use alone those goods which God gave in common; by not giving to others that which they themselves received, they become homicides and murderers, inasmuch as in keeping for themselves those things which would have alleviated the sufferings of the poor, we may say that they every day cause the death of as many persons as they might have fed and did not. When, therefore, we offer the means of living to the indigent, we do not give them anything of ours but that which of right belongs to them. It is less a work of mercy that we perform than the payment of a debt.

—ST. GREGORY THE GREAT.

Your predecessors, said Saint Simon, addressing his Holiness the Pope, have sufficiently perfected and propagated the theology of Christianity. It is now your duty to attend to the application of its doctrines. True Christianity should render men happy not only in Heaven but also on earth. Let your task consist in organising the human species according to the fundamental principle of divine morality. You must not limit your action to reminding the faithful that the poor are the beloved children of God, but must boldly and energetically employ all the power and the means of the militant Church to bring about a speedy improvement in the moral and physical condition of the most numerous class.

—ST. SIMON.

If the great end of life were to multiply yards of cloth and cotton twist, and if the glory of England consists or consisted in multiplying without stint or limit these articles and the like at the lowest possible price, so as to undersell all the nations of the world, well, then, let us go on. But if the domestic life of the people be vital above all; if the peace, the purity of homes, the education of children, the duties of wives and mothers, the duties of husbands and fathers, be written in the natural law of mankind, and if these things be sacred, far beyond anything that can be sold in the market, then I say, if the hours of labour resulting from the unregulated sale of man's strength and skill shall lead to the destruction of domestic life, to the neglect of children, to the turning of wives and mothers into living machines, and of fathers and husbands into – what shall I say, creatures of burden? – I will not use any other word, who rise up before the sun and come back when it is set, wearied, and able only to take food and lie down to rest; the domestic life of men exists no longer, and we dare not go on in this path.

—Cardinal MANNING.

Unhappy ones that you the rich are! what answer will you make to the Great Judge? You cover with tapestry the bareness of your walls, and do not clothe the nakedness of men. You adorn your steeds with most rich and costly trappings, and despise your brother who is in rags. You allow the corn in your granaries to rot or to be eaten up by vermin, and you deign not even to cast a glance on those who have no bread. You hoard your wealth, and do not deign to look upon those who are worn and oppressed by necessity! You will say to me: "What wrong do I commit if I hoard that which is mine?" And I ask you: "Which are the things that you think belong to you? From whom did you receive them? You act like a man who being in a theatre, and having seized upon the places that others might have taken, seeks to prevent every one else from entering, applying to his own use that which should be for the use of all." And thus it is with the rich, who, having been the first to obtain possession of those things which should be common to all, appropriate them to themselves and retain them in their possession; for if each one took only what is necessary for his subsistence, and gave the rest to the indigent, there would be neither rich nor poor.

—ST. BASIL THE GREAT.

You received your fortune by inheritance; so be it! Therefore you have not sinned personally, but how know you that you may not be enjoying the fruits of theft and crime committed before you?

—ST. JOHN CHRYSOSTOM.

In the beginning of the world there were no bondmen; and no man ought to become bond unless he has done treason to his Lord – such treason as Lucifer did to God. But you and your lords, good people, are neither angels nor spirits; but both you and they are men – men formed in the same similitude. Why then should you be kept like brute beasts? And why if you labour should you have no wages? Again, good people, things will never go well in England so long as goods be not in common, and so long as there be villeins and gentlemen. By what right are they whom men call lords greater folk than we? On what ground have they deserved it? If all came from the same father and mother, Adam and Eve, how can they say or prove that they are better than we, if it be not that they make us gain for them by our toil what they spend in their pride. They are clothed in velvet and are warm in their furs and ermines while we are covered in rags. They have wine and spices and fair bread, and we oatcake and straw and water to drink. They have leisure and fine houses; we have pain and labour – the wind and rain in the fields; and yet it is of us and of our toil that these men hold their state.

—JOHN BALL, "The Mad Priest of Kent," 1381.

If we define altruism as being all action, which, in the normal course of things, benefits others instead of benefiting self, then from the dawn of life altruism has been no less essential than egoism.

—HERBERT SPENCER.

The holder of a monopoly is a sinner and offender. The taker of interest and the giver of it, and the writers of its papers and the witnesses of it, are all equal in crime.

—MOHAMMED.

This system of unchecked competition – one cannot repeat it too often – means a prodigal and frightful waste. Some have to work too hard and too long; others cannot get any work to do at all or get it irregularly and uncertainly; others who might work do not and will not – the idlers at both ends of the social scale, the moral refuse produced by our economic system. This system is exactly what we find in nature generally: but one would think that human beings might use their reason to discover some less wasteful scheme.

—Professor D. G. RITCHIE, Author of
Darwinism and Socialism, &c.

At first sight it seems true that character has not been put in the foreground of Socialist discussion; its emphasis appears to be laid almost exclusively on machinery, on a reconstruction of the material conditions and organisation of life. But machinery is a means to an end, as much to a Socialist as to any one else; and the end, at any rate as conceived by the Socialist, is the development of human nature in scope, powers of life and enjoyment ... The forces required to work Collectivist machinery are nothing if not moral; and so we also hear the complaint that Socialists are too ideal, that they make too great a demand upon human nature and upon the social will and imagination. Of the two complaints this is certainly the most pertinent. A conception, however, which is liable to be dismissed, now as mere mechanism, now as mere morality, may possibly be working toward a higher synthesis ... If institutions depend on character, character depends on institutions; it is upon their necessary interaction that the Socialist insists.

—SIDNEY BALL, *Oxford*.

The animal species in which individual struggle has been reduced to its narrowest limits, and the practice of mutual aid has attained the greatest development, are invariably the most numerous, the most prosperous, and the most open to further progress.

—P. KROPOTKIN.

If we are still reminded that only through struggle can mankind attain any good thing, let us remember that there is a struggle from which we can never altogether escape – the struggle against nature, including the blind forces of human passion. There will always be enough to do in this ceaseless struggle to call forth all the energies of which human nature at its very best is capable. At present how much of these energies, intellectual and moral as well as physical, is wasted in mutual destruction? May we not hope that by degrees this mutual conflict will be turned into mutual help? And, if it is pointed out that even at present mutual help does come about, even through mutual conflict, indirectly and with much loss on the way, may we not hope to make that mutual help conscious, rational, systematic, and so to eliminate more and more the suffering going on around us?

—Professor RITCHIE.

The teaching of reason to the individual must always be that the present time and his own interests therein are all-important to him. Yet the forces which are working out our development are primarily concerned not with those interests of the individual, but with those widely different interests of a social organism subject to quite other conditions and possessed of an indefinitely longer life ... The central fact with which we are confronted in our progressive societies is, therefore, that the interests of the social organism and those of the individuals comprising it at any time are actually antagonistic; they can never be reconciled; they are inherently and essentially irreconcilable.

—BENJAMIN KIDD.

The process of social development which has been taking place, and which is still in progress in our Western civilisation, is not the product of the intellect, but the motive force behind it has had its seat and origin in the fund of altruistic feeling with which our civilisation has become equipped. The survival of the fittest, of course, does not mean the survival of the strongest, it means the survival of the adapted – the survival of the most fitted to the circumstances which surround it. A fish survives in water when a leaking ironclad goes to the bottom, not because it is stronger, but because it is better adapted to the element in which it lives. A Texas bull is stronger than a mosquito, but in an autumn drought the bull dies, the mosquito lives. Fitness to survive is simply fittedness, and has nothing to do with strength, or courage, or intelligence, or cunning as such, but only with adjustments as fit or unfit to the world around ... Men begin to see an undeviating ethical purpose in this material world – a tide, that from eternity has never turned, making for perfectness. In that vast progression of Nature, that vision of all things from the first of time moving from low to high, from incompleteness to completeness, from imperfection to perfection, the moral nature recognises in all its height and depth the eternal claim upon itself.

—Professor DRUMMOND.

Man, no doubt, is very weak: he is still a long way from being perfect. No doubt the coarse instincts of the beast are still alive in him, for he has freed himself from brute-like existence only by long and constant efforts, and animality has by no means lost its hold. But by a long course of steady progress, ever more and more conscient, he has improved his condition, and in future ages he will do so to a much greater extent.

—CH. LETOURNEAU.

A great nation does not mock Heaven and its powers by pretending belief in a revelation which asserts the love of money to be the root of all evil, and declaring at the same time that it is actuated, and intends to be actuated, in all their national deeds and measures by no other love.

—JOHN RUSKIN.

CHAPTER 5

I contend that from 1563 to 1824, a conspiracy, concocted by the law and carried out by parties interested in its success, was entered into, to cheat the English workman of his wages, to tie him to the soil, to deprive him of hope, and to degrade him into irremediable poverty.

—THOROLD ROGERS.

Hitherto it is questionable if all the mechanical inventions yet made have lightened the day's toil of any human being. They have enabled a great population to live the same life of drudgery and imprisonment, and an increased number of manufacturers, and others, to make large fortunes ... To work at the bidding and for the profit of another without any interest in the work – the price of their labour being adjusted by hostile competition, one side demanding as much, and the other paying as little, as possible – is not, even when wages are high, a satisfactory state for human beings of educated intelligence, who have ceased to think themselves naturally inferior to those whom they serve.... The objection ordinarily made to a system of community of property and equal distribution of the produce, that each person would be incessantly occupied in evading his fair share of the work, points, undoubtedly, to a real difficulty. But those who urge this objection forget to how great an extent the same difficulty exists under the system on which nine-tenths of the business of society is now conducted. The objection supposes that honest and efficient labour is only to be had from those who are themselves individually to reap the benefit of their own exertions. But how small a part of all the labour performed in England, from the lowest paid to the highest, is done by persons working for their own benefit. From the Irish reaper or hodman to the Chief Justice or the Minister of State, nearly all the work of society is remunerated by day wages or fixed salaries. A factory operative has less personal interest in his work than a member of a Communist association, since he is not, like him, working for a partnership of which he is himself a member ...

But these difficulties, though real, are not necessarily insuperable. The apportionment of work to the strength and capacities of individuals, the mitigation of a general rule to provide for cases in which it would operate harshly, are not problems to which human intelligence, guided by a sense of justice, would be inadequate. And the worst and most unjust arrangement which could be made of these points, under a system aiming at equality, would be so far short of the inequality and injustice with which labour (not to speak of remuneration) is now apportioned, as to be scarcely worth counting in the comparison. We must remember too that Communism, as a system of society, exists only in idea; that its difficulties, at present, are much better under-stood than its resources; and that the intellect of mankind is only beginning to contrive the means of organising it in detail, so as to overcome the one and derive the greatest advantage from the other.

If, therefore, the choice were to be made between Communism with all its chances, and the present state of society with all its sufferings and injustices; if the institution of private property necessarily carried with it as a consequence, that the produce of labour should be apportioned as we now see it, almost in an inverse ratio to the labour – the largest portions to those who have never worked at all, the next largest to those whose work is almost nominal, and so in a descending scale, the remuneration dwindling as the work grows harder and more disagreeable, until the most fatiguing and exhausting bodily labour cannot count with certainty on being able to earn even the necessaries of life – if this or Communism were the alternative, all the difficulties, great or small, of Communism would be but as dust in the balance.

—JOHN STUART MILL.

To me, at least, it would be enough to condemn modern society as hardly an advance on slavery or serfdom, if the permanent condition of industry were to be that which we behold, that 90 per cent. of the actual producers of wealth have no home that they can call their own beyond the end of the week; have no bit of soil, or so much as a room that belongs to them; have nothing of value of any kind except as much old furniture as will go in a cart; have the precarious chance of weekly wages which barely suffice to keep them in health; are housed for the most part in places that no man thinks fit for his horse; are separated by so narrow a margin from destitution that a month of bad trade, sickness, or unexpected loss brings them face to face with hunger and pauperism ... This is the normal state of the average workman in town or country.

—FREDERIC HARRISON.

It is mainly to our industry that we owe our greatness. Now, our industrial productions, so exuberant and so complex, result principally from our ingenious implements and from our external division of labour. But this *crumbling* of mechanical labour has a most disastrous effect upon the general development of the intelligence. It has come from the formation of an ever-increasing class of modern workmen who have no time to think or to instruct themselves. Owing to this state of things we see crying inequalities in the various conditions of our social welfare and of our knowledge. These are fearful plagues in our civilisation; they are blots which all free and intelligent societies of men ought to endeavour to remedy.

—CH. LETOURNEAU.

Ye sheep without shepherd, it is not the pasture that has been shut from you, but the Presence. Meat! perhaps your right to that may be pleadable; but other rights have to be pleaded first. Claim your crumbs from the table if you will; but claim them as children, not as dogs; claim your right to be fed, but claim more loudly your right to be holy, perfect, and pure.

Strange words to be used of working people! What! holy; without any long robes or anointing oils; these rough-jacketed, rough-worded persons; set to nameless, dishonoured service! Perfect! these with dim eyes and cramped limbs, and slowly wakening minds? Pure! these, with sensual desire and grovelling thought; foul of body and coarse of soul? It may be so; nevertheless, such as they are, they are the holiest, perfectest, purest persons the earth can at present show. They may be what you have said; but if so, they yet are holier than we who have left them thus.

—JOHN RUSKIN.

CHAPTER 6

It is often argued that the possession of the suffrage is of very infinitesimal value to the poor man and will do very little good to the poor woman when she gets it. What is a vote to those who are in want of bread? A vote is not merely an occasional and indirect means of exerting a small fraction of political influence, but, what is much more important, it is a stamp of full citizenship, of dignity and of responsibility. It is a distinct mark that the possessors of it can no longer be systematically ignored by governments, and can no longer shirk the duty of thinking about public and common interests ... There is another alternative, and that is the socialistic. The elevation of the status of women and the regulations of the conditions of labour are ultimately inseparable questions.

—Professor RITCHIE.

The restraints of Communism would be freedom in comparison with the present condition of the majority of the human race. The generality of labourers in this and most other countries have as little choice of occupation or freedom of locomotion, are practically as dependent on fixed rules and on the will of others, as they could be on any system short of actual slavery; to say nothing of the entire domestic subjection of one half the species, to which it is the signal honour of Owenism and most other forms of Socialism that they assign equal rights, in all respects, with those of the hitherto dominant sex. But it is not by comparison with the present bad state of society that the claims of Communism can be estimated.

—J. S. MILL.

There has arisen in society a figure which is certainly the most mournful and in some respects the most awful upon which the eye of the moralist can dwell. That unhappy being whose very name is a shame to speak; who counterfeits with a cold heart the transports of affection, and submits herself as the passive instrument of lust; who is scorned and insulted as the vilest of her sex, and doomed for the most part to disease and abject wretchedness and an early death, appears in every age as the perpetual symbol of the degradation and the sinfulness of man. Herself the supreme type of vice, she is ultimately the efficient guardian of virtue. But for her the unchallenged purity of countless happy homes would be polluted, and not a few who, in the pride of their untempted chastity, think of her with an indignant shudder would have known the agony of remorse and despair. In that one degraded and ignoble form are concentrated the passions that might have filled the world with shame. She remains, while creeds and civilisations rise and fall, the eternal priestess of humanity, blasted for the sins of the people.

—LECKY, Author of *History of Civilisation.*

The various forms of Communism are compatible with the most diverse kinds of general intercourse, but not with one kind – venal love. Where there is no production of commodities for sale, where nothing is bought or sold, the body of woman, like the power to work, ceases to be saleable ware.

—KARL KAUTSKY, Author of *Communism in Central Europe during the time of the Reformation,* &c.

CHAPTERS 7–8

To fill this little island with true friends – men brave, wise, and happy! Is it so impossible, think you, after the world's eighteen hundred years of toil, to fill only this little white gleaming crag with happy creatures, helpful to each other? Africa and India, and the Brazilian wide-watered plain, are these not wide enough for the ignorance of our race? Have they not space enough for its pain? Must we remain *here* also savage, – *here* at enmity with each other, – *here* foodless, houseless, in rags, in dust, and without hope, as thousands and tens of thousands of us are lying? Do not think it, gentlemen. The thought that it is inevitable is the last infidelity; infidelity not to God only, but to every creature and every law that He has made. Are we to think that the earth was only shaped to be a globe of torture, and that there cannot be one spot of it where peace can rest or justice reign? Where are men ever to be happy, if not in England? By whom shall they ever be taught to do right, if not by you? Are we not of a race first among the strong ones of the earth; the blood in us incapable of weariness, unconquerable by grief? Have we not a history of which we can hardly think without becoming insolent in our just pride of it?

And this is the race, then, that we know no more how to govern! and this the history which we are to behold broken off by sedition! and this is the country, of all others, where life is to become difficult to the honest, and ridiculous to the wise! and the catastrophe, forsooth, is to come just when we have been making swiftest progress beyond the wisdom and wealth of the past. Our cities are a wilderness of spinning-wheels instead of palaces; yet the people have not clothes. We have blackened every leaf of English greenwood with ashes, and the people die of cold; our harbours are a forest of merchant ships, and the people die of hunger.

—JOHN RUSKIN.

A gradual allotment of the primitive common domain, then an inverse movement involving the concentration of these allotments in the hands of a small number of large proprietors: this is the general formula of the evolution of property. The communal system is destroyed by the individualistic instinct; then the great eat up the small; whence languor, sickness, and death of the social body. It has been thus with the nations which have run through all the phases of their historic existence.

—CH. LETOURNEAU.

It may well be the case, and there is every reason to fear it is the case, that there is collected a population in our great towns which equals in amount the whole of those who lived in England and Wales six centuries ago, but whose condition is more destitute, whose homes are more squalid, whose means are more uncertain, whose prospects are more hopeless, than the poorest serfs of the Middle Ages or the meanest drudges of the mediaeval cities.

—Professor THOROLD ROGERS.

Society, like art, is a part of nature; but it is convenient to distinguish those parts of nature in which man plays the part of immediate cause as something apart; and, therefore, society, like art, is usefully to be considered as distinct from nature. It is the more desirable, and even necessary, to make this distinction, since society differs from nature in having a definite moral object; whence it comes about that the course shaped by the ethical man – the member of society or citizen – necessarily runs counter to that which the non-ethical man – the primitive savage, or man as a mere member of the animal kingdom – tends to adopt. The latter fights out the struggle for existence to the bitter end like any other animal; the former devotes his best energies to the object of setting limits to the struggle. The history of civilisation – that is, of society – is the record of the attempts which the human race has made to escape from this position (i.e. the struggle for existence in which those who were best fitted to cope with their circumstances, but not the best in any other sense, survived). The first men who substituted the state of mutual peace for that of war, whatever the motive which impelled them to take that step, created society. But in establishing peace, they obviously put a limit upon the struggle for existence. Between the members of that society, at any rate, it was not to be pursued à *outrance*. And of all the successive shapes which society has taken, that most nearly approaches perfection in which war of individual against individual is most strictly limited.

—Professor HUXLEY.

There is no wealth but life, including all its powers of love, of joy, and of admiration. That country is the richest which nourishes the greatest numbers of noble and happy human beings; that man is richest who, having perfected the functions of his own life to the utmost, has also the widest helpful influence, both personal and by means of his possessions, over the lives of others ... Nevertheless, it is open, I repeat, to serious question, which I leave to the reader's pondering, whether among national manufactures that of souls of a good quality may not at last turn out a quite leadingly lucrative one? Nay, in some far-away and yet undreamt-of hour, I can even imagine that England may cast all thoughts of possessive wealth back to the barbaric nations among whom they first arose; and that, while the sands of the Indus and adamant of Golconda may yet stiffen the housings of the charger, and flash from the turban of the slave, she, as a Christian mother, may at last attain to the virtues and treasures of a heathen one, and be able to lead forth her sons, saying— "These are my jewels."

—JOHN RUSKIN.

BIBLIOGRAPHY

A Selection of Writings for the guidance of those who desire to learn more about Socialism and the Modern Labour Movement.

CAPITAL. By Karl Marx. (Sonnenschein.)

CIVILISATION: ITS CAUSE AND CURE. By Edward Carpenter. (Swan Sonnenschein & Co.)

POVERTY; A STUDY OF TOWN LIFE. By B. S. Rowntree. (Macmillan & Co.)

RICHES AND POVERTY. By L. G. Chiozza Money. (Methuen & Co.)

SOCIALISM: ITS GROWTH AND OUTCOME. By William Morris and E. Belfort Bax. (Swan Sonnenschein & Co.)

COMMUNISM IN CENTRAL EUROPE IN THE TIME OF THE REFORMATION. By Karl Kautsky. (T. Fisher Unwin.)

UNTO THIS LAST. By John Ruskin. (George Allen.)

NEWS FROM NOWHERE. By William Morris. (Reeves.)

SOCIALISM AND SOCIETY. By J. Ramsay Macdonald, M.P. (Independent Labour Party.)

MERRIE ENGLAND. By Robert Blatchford. *Clarion* Office.

HISTORICAL BASIS OF SOCIALISM IN ENGLAND. H. M. Hyndman.

COMMERCE AND CHRISTIANITY. By A. B. Killin.

STUDIES IN SOCIALISM. By Jean Jaures. (Independent Labour Party.)

THE ASCENT OF MAN. By Henry Drummond. (Hodder & Stoughton.)

TOWN LIFE IN THE FIFTEENTH CENTURY. By Alice Stopford Green. (Macmillan & Co.)

THE CROWN OF WILD OLIVE. By Ruskin. (George Allen.)

THE ECONOMIC INTERPRETATION OF HISTORY. By J. E. Thorold Rogers. (T. Fisher Unwin.)

SOCIOLOGY. By Ch. Letourneau. (Chapman & Hall.)

MUTUAL AID. By P. Kropotkin. (Heinemann.)

PROPERTY: ITS ORIGIN AND DEVELOPMENT. By Ch. Letourneau. (Walter Scott.)

INDUSTRIAL DEMOCRACY. By Webb. (Longmans & Co.)

DARWINISM AND POLITICS. By D. G. Ritchie (Swan Sonnenschein & Co.)

THE LABOUR MOVEMENT. By L. T. Hobhouse, M.A. (T. Fisher Unwin.)

PAST AND PRESENT. Thomas Carlyle.

PROGRESS AND POVERTY. Henry George.

THE NEW CRUSADE. By A. G. Sparrow.